Farming the City
Food as a Tool for Today's Urbanisation

Edited by **CITIES**

....

trancity×valiz

Introduction

Section 1
The Food Field and the Food Policy Discipline

Section 2
Food Economies and Their Relationship with a New Social Topography

Section 3
Urban Society;
Citizens, Artists
and Activists

The Selection

Epilogue

35 projects

....

AgroCulture Nomadi
112

Agrowculture.org
116

Almere Oosterwold
117

B-line
120

....

....

....

....

Common Good City Farm
134

Culinary Misfits
138

Dakboerin
142

DemoTuinNoord
144

....

....

....

....

Good Food Jobs
154

Helsinki Plant Tram
158

HK Farm
162

Incredible Edible Todmorden
166

....

....

....

....

R-Urban
176

Rijp en Groen Tolsteeg
178

Roppongi Nouen Farm
182

Sky Greens
186

....

....

....

....

UIT JE EIGEN STAD
196

Varkenshuis
200

Zuidpark
202

Preface

Local food systems have the potential to catalyse change: community-based food production, processing, distribution and consumption initiatives can work together to improve economic, environmental and social outcomes. Taking this approach, *Farming the City* defines the relationship between food and the city in a holistic way. This book represents our efforts to create shared visions, a shared vocabulary, and a degree of cohesion between individuals and organisations that traditionally do not interact well. Cultural change at this level is risky and much is at stake; raising awareness and discussing the issues is always a necessary first step.

Our journey into local food systems and their potential positive impact on society has brought us into contact with a great many activists and thinkers behind the truly inspirational range of ingenious and innovative projects taking place across the urban food field. This incredible display of activity led us to realise that our work presented the perfect opportunity to 'join the dots' and map the new space in which these cultural entrepreneurs are operating.

This book outlines ways of using food as a tool to approach the many challenges inherent in contemporary urban life from a human, locally-oriented perspective. It aims to trace a path towards a socially, culturally and economically resilient society; a place where inclusive, locally-oriented modes of production are not only possible, but preferable.

Editorial

This book is a compilation of explanations, insights, case studies, exemplars and critical analysis from practitioners and experts in the food field. Needless to say, we could not put together a book about food as a tool for urban development without inviting Carolyn Steel, UK-based architect and author of *Hungry City: How Food Shapes Our Lives*, to set the parameters. In her introduction to *Farming the City – the Book*, Steel describes a perplexing urban paradox: 'The closer we cluster together, the further removed we get from our sources of sustenance'. She suggests that the city – in fact the world – is defined by its relationship with food; a process she labels 'sitopia':

'The first thing we need to do is to stop seeing cities as inert objects and recognise them as organic entities, inextricably bound to the natural ecosystem', she writes. For Steel, Sitopia, from the ancient Greek words sitos (food) and topos (place), is a way of recognising the central role that food plays in our lives, and of harnessing its potential to shape the world in a more equitable and productive way.

The book progresses by further mapping emerging territory: the food field and food planning. Kevin Morgan, Professor of Governance and Development in the School of Planning and Geography at Cardiff University, UK, introduces the notion of food discipline (not a strict diet regime, but a new field of urban studies). Pim Vermeulen, Senior Planner of the City of Amsterdam Physical Planning Department (DRO), outlines the challenges and the possibilities of generating food policy at the municipal level. Jan Jongert of 2012Architecten addresses urban infrastructure, cycles and flows; Paul de Graaf from Edible Rotterdam defines a new role for urban designers, based on the importance of understanding natural processes when creating new urban farming practice. To conclude this section, architects

Bohn and Viljoen – founders of the concept of Continuously Productive Urban Landscapes (CPUL) – discuss this revolutionary concept, presenting a concise overview of the relationship between food production, the urban realm, agriculture, design and food policy.

The book's second section aims to unpick the complex relationship between food economies and a new social topography: involvement and co-creation as drivers of citizen engagement. Derek Denckla, chair of Slow Money NYC, stresses the fact that connecting food advocacy and urban development is a hugely complex task, asserting the need to re-define the relevance of small farms as assets for the urban economy in terms beyond mere economic value. Dutch urban agriculture expert Jan-Willem van der Schans' overview of the structure and nature of food production, its models of reference and its spatial organisation, offers a critical analysis of the key issues. Describing and defining the role of advocacy for healthier food in low-income neighbourhoods, Dr Oran Hesterman, president and CEO of Fair Food Network, USA, analyses the potentially transformative impact of locally-focused food retailing and welfare strategies. Dr Jennifer Sumner from the Adult Education and Community Development Program at OISE/University of Toronto, Dr JJ McMurtry, Program Director of the Graduate Program in Social and Political Thought at York University, Toronto, and Michael Claessens, a PhD Candidate in York's Faculty of Environmental Studies, together address place-based social strategies for increasing food security and building alternative social infrastructure, rooted in developing and strengthening a collective sense of place.

The third section of the book explores practical strategies for supporting the development of cohesive urban communities. Artist Debra Solomon and art historian Mariska van den Berg from Urbaniahoeve outline the process of converting public green into edible green (landscapes to foodscapes). Artists Alex Wilde and Annechien Meier consider the role of artists in supporting community engagement with local social and economic issues. Designers Chris Berthelsen, Jared Braiterman and Jess Mantell discover the socially revealing fruit-producing landscapes and fruit paths of the megacity. The sad tale of how careless planning policy can negatively impact on community resilience is told by urban anthropologist Sonja Lebos. Finally, policy advisors Simone Plantinga and Floor de Sera present a useful engagement 'roadmap', outlining the key tools, processes, policies and guidelines that can help communities to secure project buy-in from policymakers and local government.

The final section of the book is an ode to invention, innovation and inspiration. The Farming the City Selection showcases 35 exemplary urban farming projects from the global north, providing valuable insight into how citizens, entrepreneurs, organisations and public officers are using food as a tool to re-interpret contemporary notions of urban living, working and collaboration.

By way of conclusion, the book's editors explore the theoretical framework of economic clustering as a concept for describing, understanding and communicating the potential of the urban 'food field': a grouping of food-related businesses, local economies and communities working within a cooperative framework. By vertically integrating production, transport, processing, packaging and waste flows into one cycle, the food field could potentially drive a coherent urban strategy guiding future urban dwellers in the transition to truly resilient lifestyles.

Sitopia and the urban paradox

Pre-occupation with food and its origins,
production, make-up and distribution,
as well as its taste and cost, has never been
greater amongst city dwellers. Across the
globe, emerging, self-reliant food networks
and economies are shaping both the
physical and social aspects of our cities.

....

Carolyn Steel

At the turn of the millennium, growing food was a marginal activity in European and North American cities; the province of a few allotment-holders, keen gardeners and ageing hippies from the 1970s. Today, urban food growing is an international craze, and a home-grown '$64 tomato' (as humorously described by William Alexander in his book of the same name) is the must-have accoutrement of every image-conscious city executive. What on earth is going on?

Urbanisation today represents one the greatest shifts in human dwelling patterns the world has ever seen. Cities are set to dominate the future, yet living in them presents a dilemma, since much of their food has lately come from elsewhere: a place we persist in calling 'the countryside', although the images conjured by such a term bear little relation to the realities of modern food production. This fluid situation may present us with a complex urban paradox, but it also offers opportunity: across the world's cities, food is coming home.

....

Feeding body and soul

The city reflects our dualistic needs as humans. We are political animals, who must feed both body and soul. In order to flourish, we need the company of others; yet the closer we cluster together, the further removed we get from our sources of sustenance. But we do not stand still. As we cohabit, we innovate.

Faced with the effects of the urban paradox, pre-occupation with food and its origins, production, make-up and distribution, as well as its taste and cost, has never been greater amongst city dwellers across the globe. As this book demonstrates, from the global south to pleasant European suburbs and across the inner city neighbourhoods of North America, food-related projects and policy are impacting on city life and plans for urban development. Emerging, self-reliant food networks and economies are shaping both the physical and social aspects of our cities.

These are not visions: they are reality, and they are happening now. Food is changing our urban practicalities. Locally-based food production, processing, distribution and consumption initiatives are supporting social equity and improving economic, environmental and social outcomes. Food really is the future for urban dwellers eager for change.

In my 2008 book *Hungry City: How Food Shapes Our Lives*, I explored the urban paradox through the lens of food. Whatever else we do in life, we've got to eat: a simple fact which has done more to shape our world than any other. I wanted to explore just how that worked, and to ask what would happen if, rather than let market forces shape our lives through food (the approach which Tim Lang, Professor of Food Policy at City University London, calls 'leave it to Tesco'), we were to use food as a tool to shape the world in better ways.

....

Invention and innovation

Hungry City begins with the invention of agriculture around 10,000 years ago in the ancient Near East, when our hunter-gatherer forbears began to experiment with a radical new foodstuff, grain. Their early farming settlements and cultivation of the land formed the dualistic relationship between city and country which has shaped civilisations ever since. Urbanity brought many benefits, but feeding cities was never easy. The success of the harvest was a constant concern, and transporting, storing, distributing, preserving, cooking and recycling food all presented their own difficulties. The mess and chaos of food were ubiquitous in the pre-industrial city, and maintaining a safe supply was the dominant concern of every civic authority.

This remained the case until the arrival of railways in the nineteenth century. Emancipated from the constraints of geography, cities began to spread, while the sights and smells of food began to disappear from their streets. Farms, which had previously been sited as close to cities as possible, were increasingly located far away, wherever natural resources and cheap labour could be most readily exploited. In North America and elsewhere, economies of scale, mechanisation, fertilisers and pesticides provided plentiful 'cheap' food (a historical first), while food manufacturers and retailers fought to seize market control through competition and mergers.

Governments looked the other way as profit margins were driven down and the industry became increasingly consolidated, with only the largest companies surviving.

Today, the dependence of cities on their rural hinterlands is all but invisible. Seasonality has been obliterated by 'eternal global summertime', and chemical fertilisers have replaced ancient gods as guarantors of soil fertility. Shoppers bamboozled by choice in their local supermarkets could be forgiven for thinking that the urban paradox has been solved; in reality, the opposite has been true.

The etymology of utopia – both a 'good place' (Gk. *eu-topos*) and 'no place' (*ou-topos*) – suggests why. The question of what makes a good life, or what form an ideal society might take, cannot be solved; yet to continue to ask such questions is profoundly human – it is, as Socrates said, 'the very best thing that a man can do'. If we agree, we face another quandary: how, in the light of paradox, can we ask such questions meaningfully?

In the final chapter of *Hungry City*, I coined the term *sitopia*, or food-place (Greek *sitos*, food + topos, place) to describe the world shaped by food. I suggested that sitopia could serve as an alternative to utopia as a way of addressing the dwelling problem. Unlike utopia, which seeks perfection and is thus unattainable, sitopia is already with us, albeit in a severely compromised and negative form. I suggested that, by thinking and acting through food, we could create better forms of sitopia.

....

Recognising value

Central to that idea is the question of value. Since food is essential to life and consists of living things, its value approximates to that of life itself. Food has inherent worth, which gives it unique potential as a metaphor and tool. All we need do is recognise food's true value, in order to release its creative potential.

Victor Hugo once remarked: 'The sewer is a cynic. It says everything.' Hugo was referring to the fact that nineteenth-century Parisians were more preoccupied with the image of their city than with the nutrients its sewers flushed away. What would a contemporary Hugo think, one wonders, of a society in which the calories available per head were nearly twice those needed for a healthy life, and half the food was wasted? Or in which one third of the population were obese and one seventh lived on food stamps? Or in which one in five meals was *eaten in a car*?

The USA is the world's foremost industrialised food culture and leading exponent of neoliberal capitalism, and offers clear examples of why food and politics can never be considered in isolation. With a food system this dystopian, it is no accident that the USA has also led the world in the search for alternatives. Green markets, organic box schemes, food co-ops, Community Supported Agriculture (CSA), neighbourhood composting, food planning and vertical farming are just some of the North American-led initiatives which make up the so-called 'Food Movement' now spreading throughout the developed world.

Ostensibly about food, this movement is really more akin to an informal political party. Food, after all, shaped every society on earth, and sharing its challenges led to the cooperation and trust, communication and language, love and sacrifice without which society could not exist.

The democratisation of food is essential, not just to global political stability, but to addressing the wider injustices and destruction caused by the current food system. But thinking and acting through food is not just about protest. It is about rediscovering our relationship with the natural world, and the value, and pleasure, of living in harmony with it. Responding to the changing of seasons, the smell of earth, the taste of good food, the company of friends and family, working with our hands, growing, cooking, appreciating and sharing food with love cost us nothing, other than the willingness to seek a life lived well.

Since *Hungry City* was published in 2008, I have met many real-life sitopians: extraordinary people already working to use food's influence to transform the world in a positive way. They include farmers, chefs, market traders, shopkeepers, architects, designers, planners, politicians, campaigners, artists, economists, students, fathers, mothers and children. They are all inspirational and I am sure many of them will feature in this book.

According to Plato, the art of asking proper questions was the point of civilisation; anyone not directly engaged in philosophy was simply making up the numbers. Ours is a different time and society, but our question – how to live a good life – remains the same. The dual dilemmas of how to survive and how to find meaning define us as human. Alone among species, it is our fate, or opportunity, to address both simultaneously.

....

Carolyn Steel is an architect, lecturer and writer, and author of *Hungry City: How Food Shapes Our Lives*

....

www.hungrycitybook.co.uk

Section 1
The Food Field and the Food Policy Discipline

Feeding the city: the challenge of urban food planning

Food planning is an important and legitimate part of the planning agenda in developed and developing countries. Feeding the city sustainably – in ways that are economically efficient, socially just and ecologically sound – is one of the quintessential challenges of the 21st century.

....

Kevin Morgan

As far as the basic essentials for life are concerned – air, water, shelter and food – urban and city planners have addressed them all, but with the conspicuous exception of food. This was the 'puzzling omission' that provoked the American Planning Association (APA) to produce its seminal *Policy Guide on Community and Regional Food Planning* in 2007.[1]

Urban planners might justify this 'puzzling omission' by claiming that the food system is largely a *rural* issue and therefore beyond the scope of the urban planning agenda. But there are two reasons as to why this argument fails to provide a convincing explanation.

First, the multifunctional character of the food system means that it impacts a variety of sectors   including public health, social justice, energy, water, land, transport and economic development – which planners already considered legitimate.

Second, food isn't only produced in a rural context. Urban agriculture has always existed in the hungry cities of the global south, and is re-appearing in the more sustainable cities of the global north, where urban designers are re-imagining 'the city as a farm'.[2]

Whatever the reasons for it, this 'puzzling omission' is now a matter of historical interest because, for the foreseeable future, food planning looks set to become an important and legitimate part of the planning agenda in developed and developing countries alike. Planners now find themselves addressing food because of the *new food equation*.[2] The new food equation refers to a number of new and highly complex developments, the most important of which are the following: rising food prices, national security, climate change, land conflicts, and rapid urbanisation.

The new food equation, and the inspiring precedent of the APA, persuaded the Association of European Schools of Planning (Aesop) to establish a new thematic group – the *Sustainable Food Planning Group* – to discuss the implications of food planning for theory, policy and practice. The first conference was held in October 2009, in the Dutch city of Almere, where Wageningen University was the local host. Stakeholders at the conference agreed that a 'food planner' could be anyone who is working in, or engaged with, the food system with the aim of rendering it more sustainable with respect to its social, economic and ecological effects.

It was necessary, at this time, to define the concept of a 'food planner' because the food planning community is profoundly diverse and multi-dimensional.[3] It is composed of every profession which has a food-related interest, as well as Non-Governmental Organisations (NGOs) that focus on social justice, public health, food security and ecological causes, all of whom are striving to make food policy making a more open and democratic process.[4]

Once confined to a narrow range of producer interests – such as agri-business, farmers and the state – food policy is slowly but surely becoming a focus for other stakeholders. Social justice and ecological integrity are the principal concerns for most people and, for this reason, there is a paradigm shift in food planning.[4]

Urban planners need to reach out to, and build alliances with, like-minded people in the city, not just in local government but across civil society too. Such alliances could help the food planning movement to connect to the most important campaigns underway in cities today, like the World Health Organization's *Healthy Cities* programme, which addresses a set of core themes every five years. The overarching goal of Phase V of the programme (2009-2013) is health equity in all local policies. This is being addressed through three core themes: caring and supportive environments, healthy living, and healthy urban design.

Though they may not be aware of it, urban planners are arguably the key players in the campaign for healthy cities because modern diseases like obesity will not be solved by the medical profession, which is largely geared to treating illness rather than promoting health.

The healthy city agenda creates two important opportunities. It gives urban planners the chance to play a more innovative role in nurturing sustainable cities, and it creates political space for the broader food planning community to put food on the policy agendas of *every* department in the municipal government. This latter message is one that has been addressed to urban leaders in developing countries for more than a decade.[5]

Weaving food into local planning policy is well underway in North America and Europe, so much so that food planning in its broadest sense is arguably one of the most important social movements of the early 21st century in the global north.

In North America and Europe, the food planning movement is finally finding its feet. While small municipalities have been the real pioneers in getting high quality food into schools and hospitals, for example, the larger city authorities have recently produced urban food strategies under the banners of public health, social justice or sustainability.

However, the greatest food planning challenges are to be found in sub-Saharan Africa and South Asia, where the least progress has been made in combating the problem of chronic hunger.[6] Significantly, the focus of the problem is changing fast: with the burgeoning of African cities, we are now witnessing the urbanisation of poverty and hunger to such a degree that cities will increasingly be in the forefront of the food planning challenge.

Paradoxically, urban planners in Africa have been part of the problem of food insecurity because, until recently, they saw it as their professional duty to rid the city of urban agriculture. The rationale for ridding the city of urban farmers and street food vendors varied from country to country, but it was often animated by a combination of sound concerns about public health and less than sound beliefs about 'urban modernity'. Thanks to the pioneering efforts of the food planning community in certain cities, especially Dar es Salaam and Kampala, urban planners are now trying to integrate local food production into the fabric of the city, helping the African city to foster rather than frustrate urban food security.

The growth of the food planning movement in both developed and developing countries has undoubtedly helped to humanise and localise the food system, not least by stressing such quality control mechanisms as provenance, traceability and trust, all of which have been debased by the 'placeless landscapes' of the agri-business sector.[7] But however laudable it may seem, localisation creates two major political problems for the food planning community.

The first concerns the *localisation* of the movement. If local focus is one of the strengths of the food planning community, it is also one of its weaknesses because, in terms of the politics of power, highly localised campaigns cannot leverage political support at national level. Their influence is simply too fragmented to be recognised. To overcome this problem, local food planning movements will need to orchestrate themselves so that they are small enough to be controlled locally, yet big enough to make a difference beyond the locality.[7]

The second issue concerns the belief that local food is better for the environment. The argument is that locally produced food is the most ecologically sustainable because it has lower food miles, thus a smaller carbon footprint. Critics of this argument rightly say that the transport of food is just one factor, and one must consider the total carbon count of the product's lifecycle.[8] What's more, sustainability cannot be reduced to a simple carbon metric because it has social and economic as well as environmental dimensions.

The social justice dimension of sustainability suggests that our greatest moral obligation today is to the poor and hungry of the world, which is why globally-sourced fairly traded produce should be treated as a legitimate component of a sustainable food system. What this means is that the food planning movement needs to embrace a *cosmopolitan* conception of sustainability in which locally produced seasonal food, and fairly traded and globally produced food, are both included.[9]

Feeding the city in a sustainable fashion – in ways that are economically efficient, socially just and ecologically sound – is one of the quintessential challenges of the 21st century. It will not be met without great political commitment to urban food planning and a bold vision for the city.

....

Kevin Morgan is Professor of Governance and Development in the School of City and Regional Planning at Cardiff University, UK

Food-steps: creating regional food chains

By implementing a more focused food policy along the regional food chain – from farming through processing, logistics, retail and catering – we can work towards creating a prosperous, sustainable and healthy city region.

....

Pim Vermeulen

Here's a question for Amsterdam city counsellors; at the most general level, what are all city dwellers most interested in? The answer is hardly controversial – the availability of seasonally independent, fresh and affordable food. Back in 1934, when the first Central Food Market was inaugurated in Amsterdam, an alderman was responsible for food supply. Today, supply is left largely to market forces. Our city urgently requires a more focused food policy, and government departments and administrators are finally responding to the need. At all levels, our policymakers are becoming more involved in the environmental, economic, health and safety aspects of the food system. With the project Proeftuin (Experimental Garden) Amsterdam (2006-2010), the city of Amsterdam highlighted local food systems as key policy issues. The aim was to combine, connect and scale up initiatives leading to the creation of a sustainable regional food supply chain; to rethink urban-rural relations and to promote healthy food, diets and lifestyles. This combination of top down and bottom-up approaches yielded positive experiences and results, outlined here, that we plan to build upon in the future.

....

Towards a sustainable food supply chain

The ambition of the Proeftuin Amsterdam programme was to stimulate all initiatives concerned with the provision of fresh and sustainable food, accessible and affordable for everyone, with due respect for our fellow human workers ('fair trade'), for livestock (animal well-being), while minimising the impact upon the environment. To realise these ambitions, a great many initiatives in the field of sustainable food, large-scale and small-scale, public and private, had to be coordinated. The issues clearly concern everyone: farmers, producers, retailers, consumers (young and old) and – last but not least – politicians and administrators.

There are four main dimensions that come to mind when thinking about these issues. Firstly, we have to acknowledge that Amsterdam is part of a worldwide supply system. Secondly, that in order to realise a more sustainable food system, we should to try to accomplish a closer co-operation between the various actors in the regional food supply chain. Thirdly, that to realise such close co-operation we should try and create more synergy between local and supra-local agricultural and horticultural stakeholders. And fourthly, that we should invest in, and profit from, a growing awareness among consumers of the origin, quality and cost of food. From each of these perspectives we can systematically look for opportunities to realise our objectives in the various stages of the regional food chain: farming, processing, logistics, retail and catering as well as consumer attitudes and behaviour.

....

A global system

Whether we think in terms of production, processing or sales, the food supply chain nowadays is both a national and an international concern. For example, it is now standard practice for farmers in Waterland (a region north of Amsterdam) to trade their extremely high milk yields (partly due to animal foods imported from South America) to a multi-national milk business – and thus serve the global market. This illustrates that the Amsterdam region is just a small link in a worldwide system. Conversely, there are African sugar-snap peas and Chilean asparagus available across Dutch and European markets. The availability of these products is a clear indication that the food system transcends seasonal cycles and takes advantage of cost-effective labour and resources elsewhere in the world.

....

Shortening the supply chain

Such on-going globalisation suggests that there is a case to be made for more extensive regionalisation of the food supply chain. A return to locally-sourced products could once again form the basis of food consumption in the Amsterdam region, leading to a more efficient use of regional production and handling processes. Such a perspective, however, confronts us with the challenge of finding sufficient space for arable farming and animal husbandry in the vicinity of the city, as well as issues with respect to the energy and water resources that are needed for food production and processing. But there are potential gains to be made in the area of logistics: shorter distances means fewer food miles.

Clearly such objectives require greater coordination between urban and rural authorities and stakeholders. An interesting development in this respect is that clean and smart technologies and innovative small-scale production methods have enabled food producers and food processing enterprises to re-settle within the compounds of the city. The Amsterdam Economic Board stimulates this development. A proactive policy, developed in close association with the region's food sector enterprises can, literally and metaphorically, provide the necessary space for the food sector to prepare itself for a new future.

....

Consumer awareness

Finding their role as food consumers too limited, critical citizens want to exercise more influence and control over their food choices in a broad sense. Tim Lang, Professor of Food Policy at City University, London, UK, identified this as the importance of 'food democracy', where every citizen has access to sustainable and healthy food. According to Lang, engagement with citizens and active knowledge sharing should be fostered in all kinds of ways, starting at home and at school. Several Proeftuin projects therefore focused on providing (healthy) lunches for children at school, a phenomenon that was, and still is, quite rare in the Netherlands. A nutritious school lunch provides more than just health-related benefits. It can increase children's concentration and therefore promote learning. At the same time, by sowing and harvesting in school working gardens, children can learn about the origins of the food they eat. In order to preserve and upscale these initiatives, more coordination between educational and health advisory bodies is required.

In Amsterdam, a growing number of young people are involved with developing food platforms and networks. These inform citizens about sustainable food systems and initiatives from abroad (for example, the Farming The City platform). But they also improve awareness of the taste and quality of everyday food (Youth Food Movement/Slow Food) and about possibilities for growing food, for example City Plot and Eatable City. Their work is much appreciated, and is gaining the support of a growing number of companies and institutions. These bottom-up developments deserve to be encouraged, and further supported.

Policy recommendations

So what are the implications for a metropolitan government wishing to make progress towards implementing a more sustainable food chain? Based on the experiences with the 'Proeftuin' programme, I can make the following recommendations.

Define food as a strategic, all-encompassing policy issue

Food systems should be high-profile policy issues, supported by all relevant municipal administrators. This is consistent with the importance of food as a strategic economic cluster as well as the urgency of health-related and environmental issues with respect to our food supply chain.

Sustainable food systems should be addressed at the regional level

The Amsterdam metropolis unites a number of cities and municipalities in the region. Clearly this necessitates communication and collaboration between all partners at the regional level. Amsterdam increasingly embraces the countryside as part of an integrated urban system. The regional countryside, with its characteristic landscapes, contributes to the quality of life of city dwellers as well as boosting the economic performance of Amsterdam. Besides being a source of local and healthy food, it offers facilities for recreation, leisure and tourism, and contributes to the regional income (GDP) by providing significant levels of employment. Efforts to realise more sustainable food chains involve both the city and the surrounding countryside; they clearly deserve a prominent place on regional and metropolitan agendas.

Stimulate farming and horticulture in and around the city;
set policy frameworks and remove restrictions and obstacles

Within the city there are a number of small-scale initiatives – around 50 to date – growing food locally, which are often the result of spontaneous bottom-up community initiatives. Most have mixed objectives, for example food growing in tandem with health awareness, social cohesion, or the education of the young and the underprivileged. Similar initiatives are also being undertaken by restaurants and offices growing vegetables on the roofs of their buildings (Zuidpark), on adjacent empty plots (restaurant Bolenius at the Zuidas) or in derelict greenhouses (restaurant De Kas and Kwekerij Osdorp). Yet these new land uses often encounter planning restrictions, thus challenging local government to devise simpler and more supportive frameworks.

Create better conditions for multifunctional farmers in peri-urban areas

The preservation of Amsterdam's much-loved peri-urban areas is highly dependent on the continuation of agricultural and horticultural activities. Amsterdam has a responsibility to create favourable conditions for such activities; an obligation that has been acknowledged by the city council through a recent policy that supports farmers in the north of Amsterdam to diversify activities and scale up their enterprises. All of this has to happen, of course, within agreed restrictions and regulations with respect to the preservation of the historical and cultural landscape.

Improve the image of vocational training institutes in the food sector

Processing companies in the seaport of Amsterdam, in the neighbouring Zaan area as well as in the Greenport and Agriport enterprises in the wider region, have problems finding qualified workers. Improving professional training in the fields of innovative and sustainable food production and processing at all educational levels is a matter of urgency.

Create better conditions for sustainable food distribution in the Amsterdam region
New logistic concepts have to be considered and investigated to make the daily delivery of food in all parts of the city more sustainable. Consumers in the city should be better connected to nearby regional and local food producers, and there are already good examples of creative intermediaries who collect fresh food from farms and deliver it to nearby retailers.

Within the built-up area of Amsterdam, the former Central Food Market (Food Centre Amsterdam) is a major wholesale distribution hub where food products are collected and then delivered to hotels, restaurants, cafés, retailers and markets in all parts of the city. Daily freight traffic to and from the city has severe environmental impacts, and the city council has demanded that plans to restructure this area should include measures to considerably reduce these impacts. The aim is to transform the Food Centre into both an attractive market place, open to the general public, and into a vibrant centre of expertise in the realm of food and food education. These are noble objectives – but they await implementation by courageous actors both in the public and the private sectors.

Encourage retail and catering companies to promote more healthy and sustainable eating habits
The retail and catering sectors should contribute towards the creation of sustainable food chains and be instrumental in promoting healthy lifestyles among citizens. Consumers should be informed about the origins of the food they eat, and invited to reflect upon the make-up of their meals. Waste, and the disposal of food and associated products, is also a key issue across all steps of the food supply chain. In this respect, restaurants can help by offering smaller portions and supplying 'doggy bags' for left-over food. Local governments should make an effort to reach agreement with the retail and catering sectors about offering such options.

Stimulate consumers to adopt both a more healthy and more sustainable lifestyle
A recent report from Amsterdam's Municipal Health Department offers alarming data on obesity and the challenges of dealing with overweight citizens. It states that 20.5 per cent of 10-year-old children are overweight, with 6.6 per cent being obese, while 29.5 per cent of those older than 16 are overweight, with 10 per cent being obese. Amsterdam's health policy focuses primarily on an 'integrated neighbourhood approach' of exercise and food programmes for children, involving schools and parents as well as the wider community. Local government should support and expand such initiatives by providing guidance and instruction, and by formulating simple and transparent rules and regulations.

....

Incremental change
Clearly, effecting changes in the food system is a daunting task. Yet what we can do is make a start by means of minor adjustments. We can change our own lifestyles, especially where local and regional governments are aware of their responsibilities in facilitating and supporting such behaviour change. We also need to encourage debate on important

ethical aspects of the food system, for example the risks and benefits of genetically modified food; the issue of animal welfare; the impacts of the use of fertilisers and pesticides; and the benefits and limitations of organic food production practices.

The Amsterdam region is surrounded by fertile lands and meadows, and enjoys advanced logistics; all favourable conditions that can be exploited. When confronted with powerful institutional players, it is the consolidation of food chain stakeholders' expertise and strengths, backed up by robust policy frameworks on the part of local and regional governments, that will encourage and enable positive change to take place.

....

Pim Vermeulen is a Senior Planner with the City of Amsterdam Physical Planning Department (DRO)

....

www.amsterdam.nl

The resilient city

The recyclicity concept envisages the re-connection of flows – food, energy, water and money – to create an integrated and regenerative process within our urban ecosytems.

....

Jan Jongert

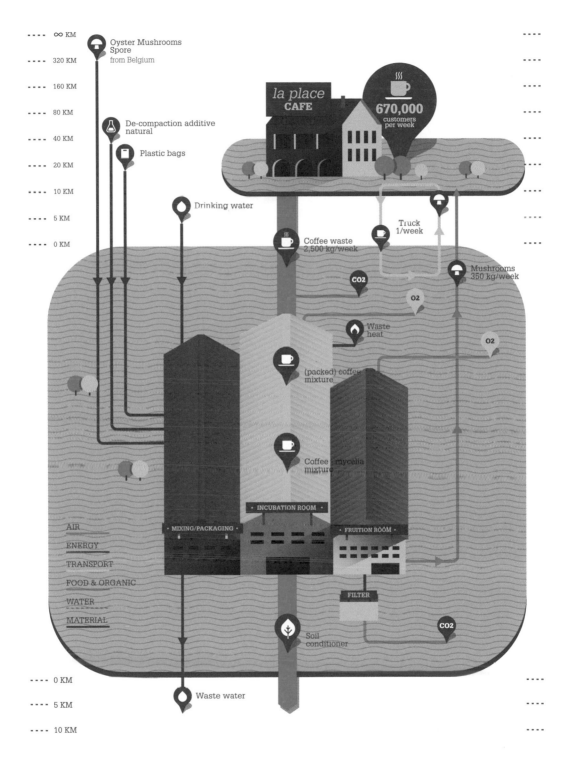

∞ KM
320 KM
160 KM
80 KM
40 KM
20 KM
10 KM
5 KM
0 KM

Oyster Mushrooms Spore
from Belgium

De-compaction additive natural

Plastic bags

Drinking water

la place
CAFE

670,000
customers per week

Coffee waste
2,500 kg/week

CO2

Truck
1/week

Mushrooms
350 kg/week

O2

Waste heat

O2

(packed) coffee mixture

Coffee : mycelia mixture

AIR
ENERGY
TRANSPORT
FOOD & ORGANIC
WATER
MATERIAL

· INCUBATION ROOM ·

· MIXING/PACKAGING ·

· FRUITION ROOM ·

FILTER

CO2

Soil conditioner

0 KM
5 KM
10 KM

Waste water

Figure 1 Case study: MSP 2040

Planning practice has, over past decades, been driven by the segregation of activities. The underlying zoning principles of land use date back to a time when different functions in rapidly growing cities had to be 'protected' from each other. During the past century, transport networks in particular have become increasingly segregated. This form of urban planning has produced inefficient cities with monofunctional zones that are largely dependent on inter-regional 'in and out flows', choking infrastructure and adding to traffic levels.

Recyclicity (Figure 2) is a strategy developed by 2012Architecten to transform these monofunctional districts into symbiotic communities that cater for all living and working needs. Disconnected flows of food, energy, water and money are replaced by an integrated and regenerative process. A successful local economy helps to strengthen civic society and empowers local communities.

To achieve such a shift away from recurring problems in our living environments, we need to focus on creating dynamic and connected processes. Our built environment is constrained by the flows it facilitates: flows of people, energy, transportation, money and knowledge. The disconnection of these flows, and the hidden nature of many, results in doubt, uncertainty and defensive behaviours from the range of stakeholders operating across each other's fields of interest.

....

The flow of food
Food, one of the primary needs for life, is a clear example of a flow that has been disconnected from our daily experience. In the urban environment, production, treatment, and storage are isolated from patterns of consumption. Waste is cleared away in closed systems such as garbage trucks and sewage pipes, with no effort to reclaim valuable materials, energy and nutrients. Profits are concentrated within large multinationals and reinvested in large-scale projects with little local context.

....

Closed versus open cycles
The growing scarceness of resources is raising awareness of the paths that our products take and the traces they leave behind, before and after use. The trends towards recycling and the closing of production loops arc logical responses, yet remain vulnerable in an era when flows can become increasingly unstable. In order to adapt flexibly to changing levels of demand and supply, it becomes necessary to create cycles with interrelated flows, dependent on multiple supply networks. Such resilient ecosystems continue to function in the event of failures. Both closed and open cycles need resilient flows. In the case of food flows, we can learn a great deal from historical examples such as the Dutch windmill, which combined several flows: harvesting wind energy, crop storage, food processing, housing for workers and a place to sell products on site. More contemporary examples are enterprises like Gro Holland that grow mushrooms using coffee waste from restaurant chains, to which it sells back the mushrooms. Taking this a step further, we are investigating the possibility of implementing similar projects in vacant buildings; using the space to grow food and converting the CO_2 from the mushroom production to energy by using the residual heat that is released in the process.

Case study: MSP 2040

In 2009, 2012Architecten began testing and researching the Cyclifier concept across three shrinking neighbourhoods in the region of Heerlen, The Netherlands. The study focused on an analysis of the metabolism of the sites; on the spatial implications of their reintegration, and the potential for energy and other flows to be short-circuited/looped. The area was formerly dependent on the mining industry, but since the closure of the pits in the 1970s, the neighbourhoods have experienced a range of socio-economic problems, including declining populations.

The design challenge lay in using the right tools to map resources and urban flows in order to create a sustainable vision for Heerlen in 2040. To achieve a connected and locally-focused city, our goal was the creation of a looped system incorporating several types of Cyclifiers. These would enable local food production, water purification, energy production and the reuse of building materials. Currently, none of these 'flows', for example energy or materials, are integrated. For example, the data indicated that none of the food produced on local farmland is processed on site. Instead, it is transported off site, processed, and transported to supermarkets. Apart from reactivating unused neighbourhood spaces, we proposed the use of Cyclifiers – greenhouses and a local bio digester – to allow food to be produced and processed within local boundaries, and water to be cleaned, stored and used on site. Locally produced photovoltaic panels would contribute 60 per cent of the electricity needed for the area. Furthermore, studying the effect on money flows, it is possible that dependency on external income in the form of social security could be reduced by an emergent local economy. The results of the study provide an interesting starting point for future research. It is already clear that there is great potential to reduce resource use from outside the local area (Figure 1).

....

The near future

The current financial crisis can be seen as creating the conditions underpinning a system transformation leading to a new kind of dynamic built environment. As money loses its primary role of representing commitment, new kinds of contracts will emerge from local groups working in creative environments rooted in the mutual benefit of real people rather than the service of market statistics. Working as an architect in such an environment means entering an exciting field that is on the verge of becoming a new multidisciplinary science. In the case of food cycles, which play such a primary role in recreating networks within functioning ecosystems, we predict that much of this science will be developed around dining tables, not boardroom tables.

....

Jan Jongert is director of 2012Architecten

....

www.2012architecten.nl

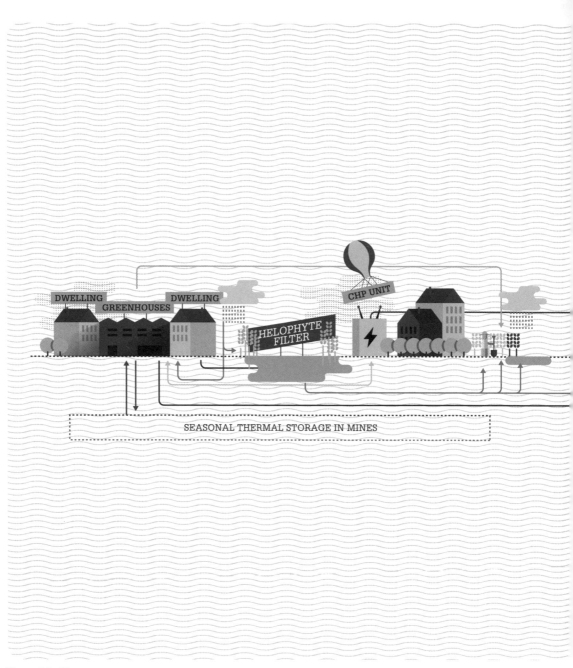

Figure 2 Cyclifier concept

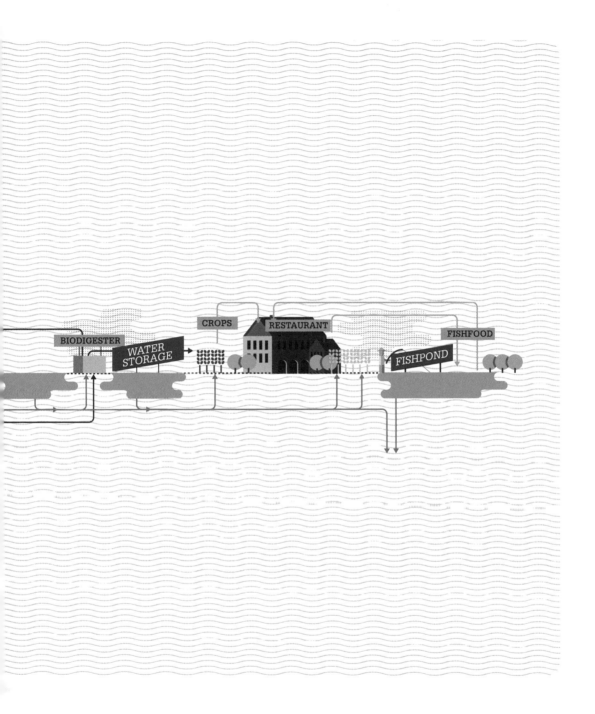

Systems thinking in practice

As the physical boundaries of our living environment are beginning to bounce back the consequences of our ever expanding lifestyle, the role of the designer will become less and less about making new artefacts, and more and more about rearranging and re-organising existing elements in more resilient and adaptable ways. Urban agriculture can help us to make the new connections our cities need.

....

Paul de Graaf

Designing for resilience requires a systems perspective; an understanding of the network of elements that constitute our living environment. Understanding this system, or network, allows us to make fundamental changes to the whole (the city) without having to fundamentally change its elements. Urban agriculture can be used as a tool for making new connections in the urban ecosystem, connecting realms such as health, food, energy, waste management and real estate, thus making the overall network more responsive and flexible.

In many developing countries, urban agriculture is both a well-established practice and a powerful, sometimes subversive, way in which citizens make the city liveable while simultaneously making a living. This potential for social empowerment, combined with environmental benefits, makes urban agriculture a tool worth investigating. It has the potential to help us re-arrange our advanced, but somewhat tired, western cities. Local food growing, within city limits, can help make cities more resilient in a positive and inclusive way.

....

Applying global knowledge locally

Of course, inspiring examples of urban agriculture practice from around the globe have to be 'translated' to suit local circumstances. In the well-to-do and highly efficient Dutch context, for example, local government is a potential ally that wants to involve citizens, improve their health and living conditions, boost the city's environmental performance and reduce maintenance costs; all potential benefits that urban agriculture can help deliver. But regulatory frameworks, silo thinking and risk-averse management practices create barriers to cross-disciplinary entrepreneurial initiative. Competition over scarce land resources – potentially with more valuable uses – makes the search for available space problematic. Finally, the prospects of making a living from urban food production are much lower in countries such as the Netherlands due to an advanced commercial agricultural sector that produces quality fresh food comparatively close to the city.

....

An unusual role for design

Successfully delivering urban agriculture projects takes daring and innovative urban farmers working with different forms of agriculture that occupy spatial and agricultural niches. Using urban agriculture as an instrument for making the city more sustainable involves designers (architects, landscape architects, urban designers and planners) developing urban planning and design strategies that support and guide urban farmers' initiatives for the benefit of the city.

First of all, these designers must understand the processes of urban agriculture, and how to work with them. Creating agricultural niches is not like applying 'green wallpaper' in different tones and textures. It is a design process that integrates water, minerals, nutrients and organic material in a system that will deliver a desired outcome, usually the cultivation of both edible and non-edible products. Urban agriculture is about facilitating these natural processes in the city; adjusting them to urban conditions, needs, wishes and desires, and enabling them to be as beneficial to the city and its inhabitants as possible.

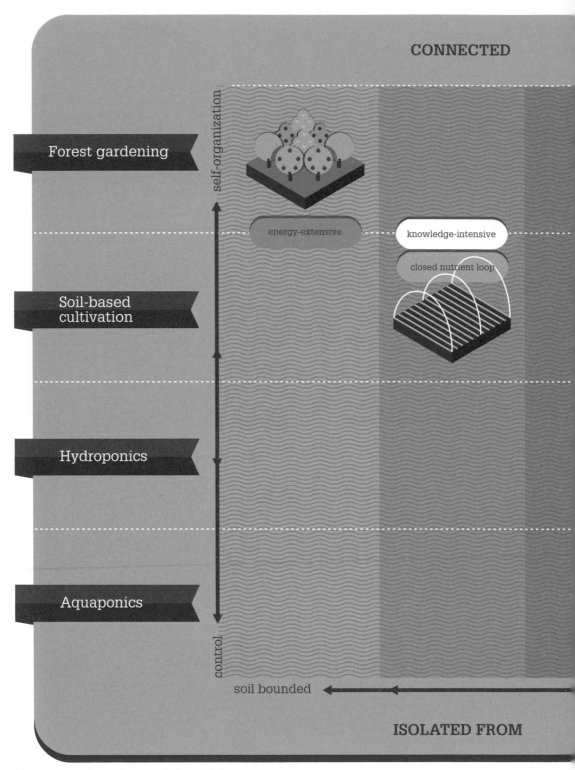

Figure 1 Matrix of promising types of urban agriculture

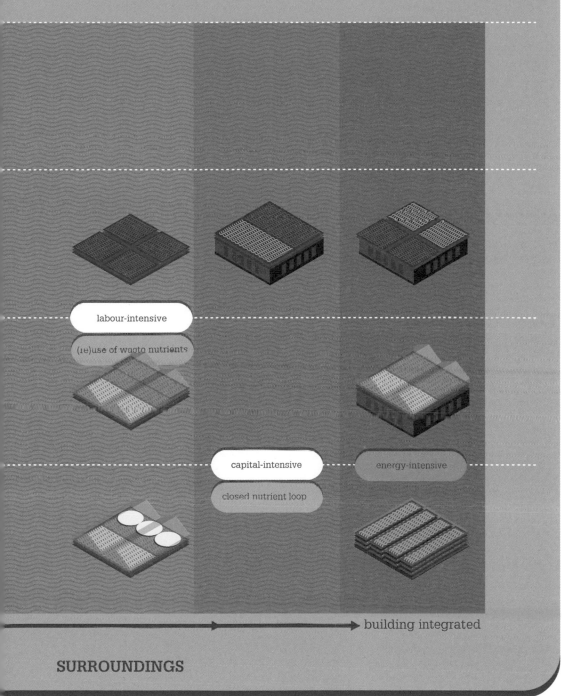

labour-intensive

(re)use of waste nutrients

capital-intensive

closed nutrient loop

energy-intensive

building integrated

Imagining the full potential of an agriculture reconfigured for an urban context requires a multidisciplinary approach, involving both agricultural experts (farmers and scientists) and urban experts (cooks, economists, retailers, housing managers, waste water managers, developers, social workers and designers). These experts, and designers in particular, do well to remain realistic about their role in the process.

Urban agriculture walks a thin line between profit and altruism. Agriculture is not a short-term, high-profit business, but one of hard work and hard-earned profit. Too many architectural renderings can stand in the way of a viable business model. The basic elements of urban agriculture (soil, plants, water, supporting structures) already have the intrinsic potential to make beautiful spaces. What urban agriculture needs, first and foremost, is the space to evolve as a practice. And to support this evolving practice, the designer has to reconsider his role.

The case of Eetbaar (edible) Rotterdam, an independent, multidisciplinary expert group on urban agriculture, formed in 2007, is a good example of such re-thinking. Eetbaar Rotterdam developed a vision of an urban agriculture that makes the city more sustainable and brings people closer to the natural food cycle. The research project *Room for urban agriculture in Rotterdam* developed an urban design strategy based on this vision, mapping opportunities for beneficial types of urban agriculture and suggesting ways to realise these opportunities (Figure 2).

....

The city: top-down and bottom-up

Urban agriculture is opportunistic by nature. It adapts to the possibilities and limitations of the city. It is driven by bottom-up initiatives and the key designers are urban farmers themselves. Traditional top-down planning and design is not appropriate here: this is understood by municipalities that wish to facilitate and stimulate urban agriculture.

However, some aspect of 'big picture' planning *is* necessary to make the whole more than the sum of its parts. Effective mapping, for example, reveals promising locations and supports the design process: which types of urban agriculture are most effective in which spaces? By mapping opportunities for urban agriculture, the municipality can help urban farmers to locate the best spaces for themselves and for the city. Good maps reflect a way of thinking and enable stakeholders to look at the city with newly informed eyes.

Finding sites for urban agriculture in the city means looking at urban space through the eyes of an urban farmer. At first glance: a landscape of asphalt, concrete, brick and soil; a range of microclimates with sunspots and shady corners, damp moist areas and dry exposed surfaces. In this landscape one can find spatial and temporal niches that are ripe for cultivation. At second sight there is another layer of opportunities hidden underneath its surface: sources of waste heat prolong the growing season, excess rain water and waste water provide irrigation and nutrition, sources of organic waste underpin the process of soil amelioration. Urban agriculture can tap these (re)sources, make good use of them and offer multiple benefits back to the city in return: turning organic waste into food and positively influencing local microclimates. Storing excess rainwater for irrigation and evaporative cooling, for example, helps to reduce midsummer heat in dense inner city areas.

Agricultural needs (Demand)	Urban supply
Sunlight / daylight	Plenty of sun-exposed surface
Nutrition / fertilizer / irrigation	Waste flows (nutrition, irrigation, substrate, heat)
Soil /substrate	
Micro-climate / environment	Micro-climate
Space	Vacant space / niche space / temporary space
Loading capacity (integrated in buildings)	Underused constructive capacity
Labour (intensive/extensive)	Labour force (employees)
Market	Customers

Urban needs (Demand)	Agricultural supply
Public green design & management	Aesthetics
Ecosystem services	Relative biodiversity
Education (nature, food production, life skills)	Experience of seasons / hands-on learning / work experience
Therapeutic work	Therapeutic work
Appropriate jobs	Skilled and unskilled labour
Water storage	Water intake & evaporation
Climate control (cooling / heating) at building and neighbourhood level	Evaporative cooling
Water improvement, soil and air quality	Purification of water, soil and air
Waste treatment and management	Organic waste treatment

Table 1 Matrices of supply and demand of agriculture and the city

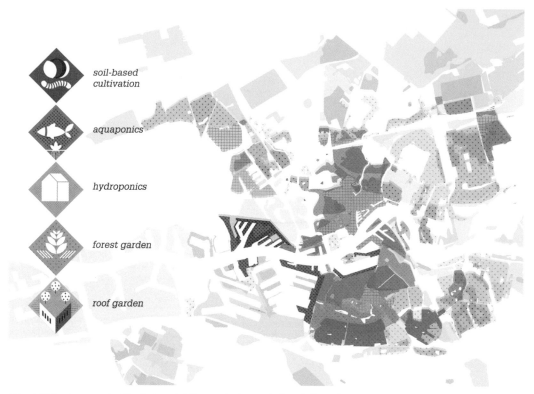

soil-based
cultivation

aquaponics

hydroponics

forest garden

roof garden

Figure 2 Mapping opportunities for beneficial types of urban agriculture in Rotterdam

Hovering over this urban landscape is a force field of laws and policies: restrictive zoning, designated areas of development and 'urban free zones' that might heighten or dampen the potential of a given space for cultivation. These layers form the spatial landscape to be mapped. Socio-cultural potential, however, involving neighbours, volunteers, customers and partners, is too dynamic to map and is better addressed directly by urban farmers in relation to their plans.

....

Mapping for diversity: distinguishing type and form

But how do we map, and plan for, the diversity of urban agriculture and its practitioners without killing it through over-classification? Examples from practice are shaped in response to local circumstances. In this light it is helpful to distinguish between types and forms, in parallel with the typology and morphology classification used in urban planning and design. In this context, a type is an abstract scheme with generic characteristics, whereas a form is a site-specific interpretation and realisation of a type; a design for a specific location for a specific urban farmer.

Types of urban agriculture are defined as cultures (ways of cultivation) or combinations of cultures (poly-cultures) complete with their defining spatial characteristics. They differ in their relation to the soil and the built environment, their relationship with the essential flows of the city, and in the impact they have on public space socially and aesthetically. Thus they offer different benefits to the city, and respond to different opportunities.

Figure 1 (see page 36) gives an overview of relevant types of professional urban agriculture; types that allow urban farmers to make a living in a city such as Rotterdam. These types match agricultural and urban needs (Table 1). Opportunities lie in reciprocal relations: agriculture that sees its needs fulfilled by the city and, by its presence, fulfils certain needs of the city. This overview is by no means comprehensive, but offers an idea of scope and diversity. It is defined by two axes that describe a 'bandwidth' ranging from control to self-organisation, and from soil-bound to building integrated. Four recurring types represent the diversity of this field.

....

Promising types of urban agriculture

One end of the spectrum is represented by forest gardening, a soil-bound and largely self-managing (outdoor) food forest. This is a small ecosystem optimised for a large and varied edible output. At the other end, we find controlled indoor substrate cultures such as hydroponics and aquaponics, with fresh produce available year-round. In between, we find more or less soil-based cultivation from ground level cultivation in full soil to raised beds, or in soil layers on rooftops. This type fits the image most people have of urban agriculture: allotment garden-style food growing.

Combined with smart cultivation schemes making use of the small spaces and microclimates of the city, allotment-style production aims to deliver fresh vegetables directly to restaurants and individuals. The familiarity of this type of urban agriculture, the wide availability of knowledge required to manage it, and the relatively low investment required make it one of the most accessible types.

Hydroponics can be seen as the high-tech version of this type. By integrating hydroponics with buildings, waste energy and waste water streams can be tapped and used, thus becoming part of the sustainable redevelopment of buildings and districts. Just like forest gardening, aquaponics works with polycultures, closing loops internally, but is also open to incorporating streams of organic waste. Aquaponics (and hydroponics) require high investment and specialised knowledge. Forest gardening requires time and a broad understanding of natural processes, cycles and interactions.

These four basic types complement each other in the products and services they deliver, in their needs and requirements, and in the way they fulfil the spatial, socio-cultural and environmental needs of the city. They represent different values: from the importance of healthy soil to the need for affordable food production in sufficient quantities. They embody very different approaches to the relationship between people and nature.

Mapping these opportunities, and weighing them according to type, reveals a diversity that translates into a variety of preferred habitats (Figure 2). These habitats are complementary and, stitched together, more or less cover the city. Instead of choosing between these approaches, each should be embraced for its particular qualities and for the diversity that a combination of types provides.

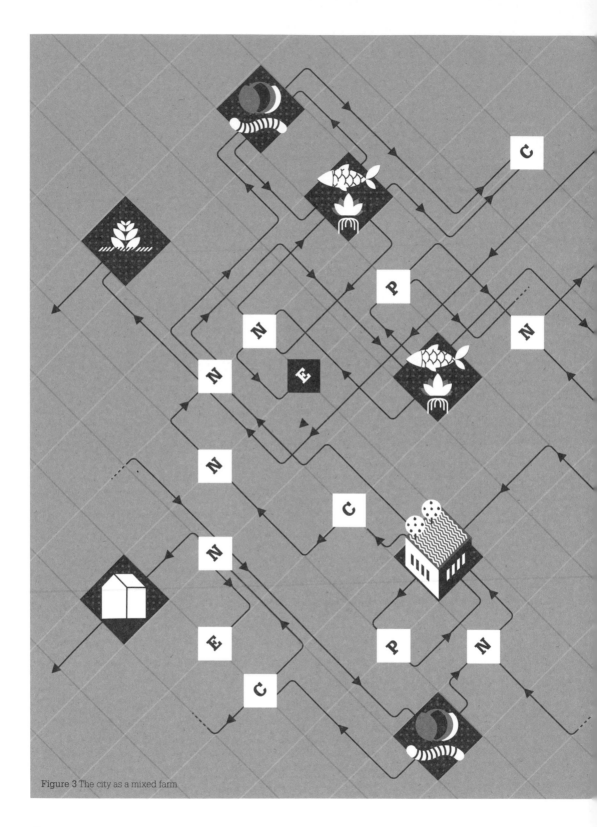

Figure 3 The city as a mixed farm

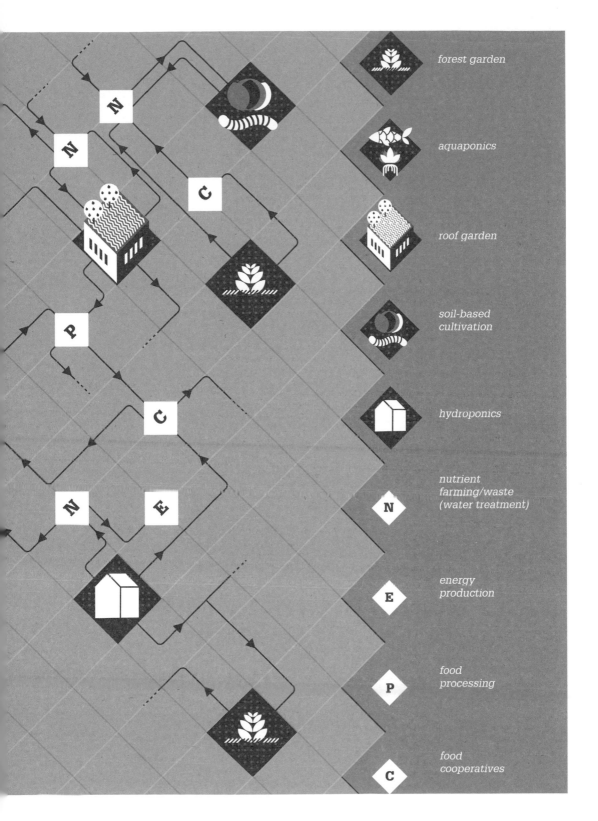

forest garden

aquaponics

roof garden

soil-based
cultivation

hydroponics

nutrient
farming/waste
(water treatment)

energy
production

food
processing

food
cooperatives

The promise of urban agriculture

From a systems perspective, the wide range of urban agriculture types is a distinct benefit, as each inhabits its own niche, serves different goals and offers a variable basis for food production. In this sense, urban agriculture becomes a way of diversifying the agricultural sector. However, as designers of the city, we should first and foremost stimulate a spectrum of forms of urban agriculture for the sake of the city; because it makes our cities better, more beautiful and more resilient places. Together the range of types – if realised on a wider scale – form a resilient network that can effectively turn a city such as Rotterdam into one big mixed farm (Figure 3). This system would be an open-ended, 'messy' system allowing for experiments, failures and competition without losing its overall capacity. Enabling and stimulating systems like these to grow is a key element of future urban design practice.

....

**Paul de Graaf is an independent researcher
and designer in the field of sustainable society
and co-founder of Eetbaar Rotterdam**

....

www.pauldegraaf.eu
www.eetbaarrotterdam.nl

Urban agriculture:
designing the productive city

Planners and activists across the globe suggest that the practice of urban cultivation is outstripping policy support. The concept of productive urban landscapes proposes a framework in which urban agriculture can contribute to more sustainable and resilient food systems.

....

Katrin Bohn and Andre Viljoen

Across the world, urban agriculture has become an increasingly common feature of cities as they respond to social, environmental and economic concerns. Commercially viable schemes of various types have been set up over the last five to ten years, complementing more established styles of urban agriculture, such as the allotments popular in Europe, or North America's community gardens.

It is possible to think of urban agriculture, to an extent, as a response to scarcity. In the modernising and developing societies of the global south, it has often been seen as a response to crisis. However, it is now being recognised as a way of *preventing* scarcity by introducing closed-loop, no-waste cultivation systems into cities, reducing food miles, providing urban heat island mitigation and creating visual amenity. There are also substantial public health and educational benefits.

....

Productive urban landscapes

Since 2005, when Bohn&Viljoen published the book *Continuous Productive Urban Landscapes* (CPULs), much has changed in relation to the practice of urban agriculture and the creation of productive urban landscapes. The CPUL City concept proposes that urban agriculture can contribute to more sustainable and resilient food systems while also benefitting the urban realm. Such a physical and environmental design strategy also provides a strategic framework for the theoretical and practical exploration of ways to implement such landscapes within contemporary urban design.[1]

Within the CPUL concept, urban agriculture refers in the main to fruit and vegetable production, as this provides the highest yields per square metre of urban ground. Key features of CPUL are outdoor spaces for food growing, shared leisure and commerce, natural habitats, non-vehicular circulation routes and ecological corridors. Its network connects existing open urban spaces, maintaining and, in some cases, modifying their current uses.[2]

In our CPUL book, we argue that urban agriculture should be integrated into city-wide networks of open space, providing a coherent and multifunctional landscape. We also suggest that the benefits are significant enough to consider CPUL as an essential, sustainable urban infrastructure. In 2005, this proposition was still seen as 'interesting' and 'utopian', but since then the situation has changed dramatically. By 2011 commentators were already defining the Dutch City of Almere's future plans for Almere Oosterwold as a CPUL.[3]

....

Getting closer to the CPUL CITY

In Almere, the objective was to explore opportunities to re-integrate agriculture into modern Dutch city life. Through an inclusive stakeholder process, a virtual city district of 250 hectares was designed, integrating living space for 5,000 inhabitants with urban agriculture.[4] The concept design highlighted urban agriculture and became integrated into Almere municipality's development plan. In January 2010, the Dutch government decided on the execution of this development plan; referred to by stakeholders as a 'unique system innovation in Dutch urban planning'.[5]

The CPUL City concept recognises that each city and each site will present a unique set of conditions and competing pressures to inform the final shape and extent of its productive landscapes. It envisages a 'mixed economy' of growers practising urban agriculture: projects for the community and by the community, small-scale and large-scale, commercial and communal.

Broadly speaking, commercial-scale production will be necessary if urban agriculture is to have a quantifiable impact on food production, whilst personalised production is very significant from a social and behaviour change perspective. It is generally acknowledged that urban agriculture will not meet all of a city's food needs, and any systematic review of urban food systems needs to consider relationships between a city, its local region and beyond.

At the time of writing, one could say (albeit in a simplified manner) that across Europe wider urban strategies that are broadly in line with the CPUL City concept are already in development. In North America, a great variety of pioneering individual projects are also underway, aiming to encompass and interlock desires for social gain, empowerment, community building, environmental improvement and commercial viability.

Baltimore, Milwaukee and Chicago are among a vanguard of North American cities actively encouraging urban agriculture. Recent discussions with planners and activists in the USA confirm our observation that practice is outstripping policy, as individuals take urban agriculture projects forward at a range of scales and with diverse aims. The range of new projects is staggering. Cuba's urban agriculture, as studied about ten years ago, revealed spatial possibilities and the effectiveness of systematic support systems, but the USA is now experimenting with models of production across the spatial, technical, organisational and financial sectors.

Across the USA, hydroponics and soil-based cultivation are being utilised for rooftop and covered (glass house) cultivation, with much work taking place in New York and Milwaukee, where practical aquaponic systems are being developed.[6] Detroit's well-publicised programme of inner city regeneration includes numerous urban agriculture initiatives, many of them small-scale, but several aim for highly ambitious commercial and social enterprises. Detroit's Eastern (food) Market, one of the few public spaces in the city, is becoming the hub for a number of urban agriculture and open space initiatives with the potential to coalesce into a CPUL space, giving coherence to a significant area of eastern Detroit.[7]

In Berlin, we are currently working on a project that reflects a specific German situation; an urban agriculture intervention with the potential to increase the social productivity of a neighbourhood. However, at the same time, this project positions itself as a component of a wider network of food-productive spaces. In this vision, developed jointly by the local council and the Technische Universität Berlin, the participatory project Spiel/Feld Marzahn[8] is a stepping stone to start an internal planning debate with the local public.[9]

Implementing CPUL
Cities across the world are seeking policy guidance, good practice examples and further evidence about the impact of urban agriculture. The London Assembly's Planning and

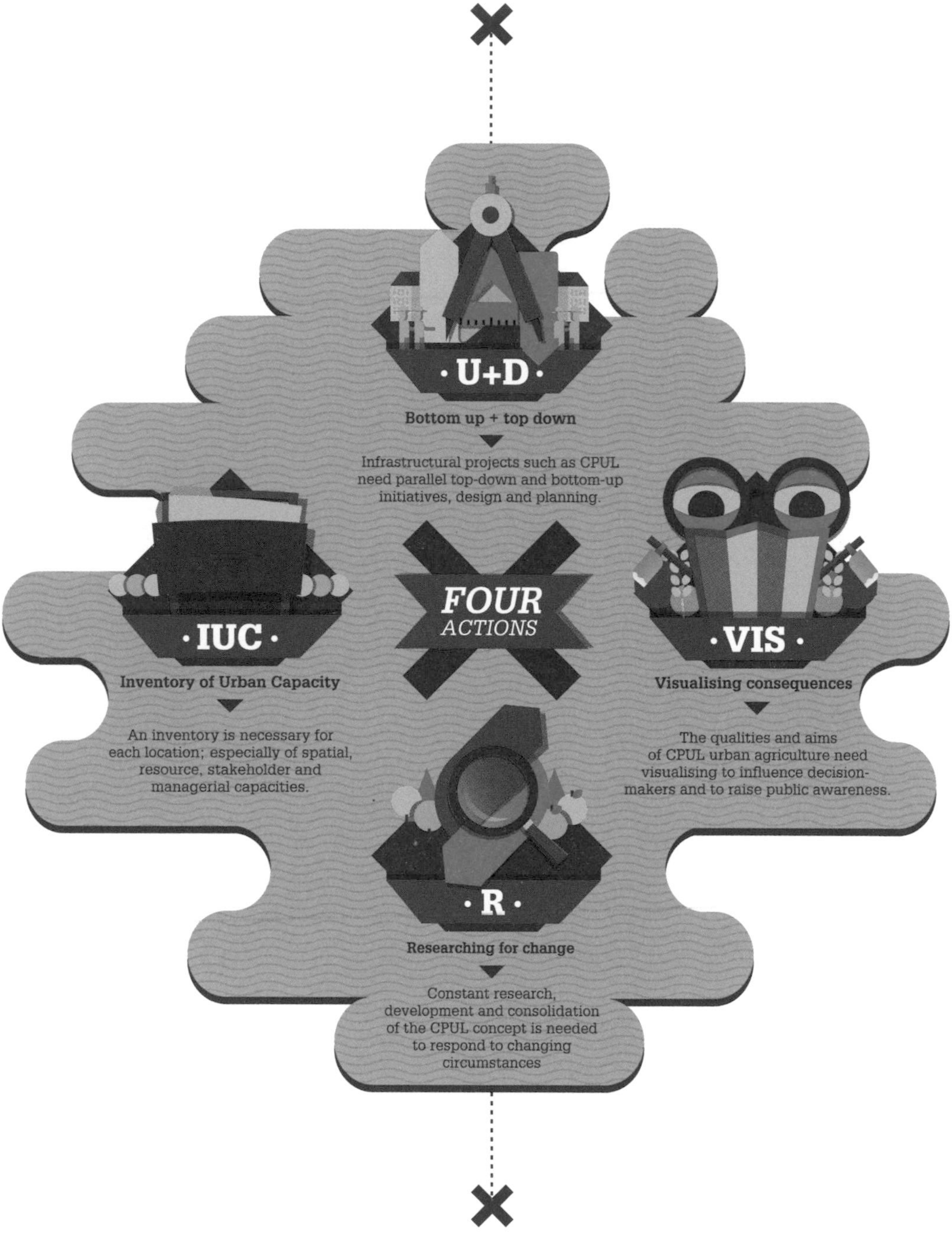

·U+D·

Bottom up + top down

Infrastructural projects such as CPUL need parallel top-down and bottom-up initiatives, design and planning.

·IUC·

Inventory of Urban Capacity

An inventory is necessary for each location; especially of spatial, resource, stakeholder and managerial capacities.

FOUR ACTIONS

·VIS·

Visualising consequences

The qualities and aims of CPUL urban agriculture need visualising to influence decision-makers and to raise public awareness.

·R·

Researching for change

Constant research, development and consolidation of the CPUL concept is needed to respond to changing circumstances

Figure 1 CPUL City Clover

Housing Committee's investigation into how the planning system could support commercial food growing in London is typical of international trends:

'Our report *Cultivating the Capital* calls for changes to the planning system to … encourage food growing in London …'.[10]

Getting urban agriculture 'written into' planning documents is the next critical enabling step everywhere in the world, along with developing a public discourse that articulates its many benefits. These range from environmental motivation through creating visual amenity to encouraging positive behaviour change; these are all actions that are required if urban agriculture is to be embedded in city frameworks and rise to the challenge of proving its value beyond direct financial return.

In Europe, the lack of policy and design guidance on urban agriculture has not prevented the establishment of successful initiatives such as the Prinzessinnengärten[11] in Berlin or the Capital Growth programme that began in London in 2009. But development can be patchy and often lacks coherence. In some cases, with Detroit being the prime example, the pursuit of differing development strategies and approaches can result in a highly contested environment, where issues of food sovereignty, political and economic approaches can polarise opinion.[12]

With this in mind, we have developed the 'CPUL City Action Plan' as a planning and design guide for implementing localised urban food systems. The action plan intends to meet the demand for systematic, practical, graphically descriptive and readily transferable know-how. Of course, many of these issues are covered elsewhere, for example in The Transition Network's book *Local Food: How to Make it Happen in Your Community*, which covers transferable information aimed at communities with committed activists.[13] Our work to date has led us to conclude that four distinct actions categorise the various tools most relevant to the architectural, urban design and planning professions. These actions acknowledge the need for interdisciplinary and transdisciplinary approaches, while also helping to define particular tasks within the competency of an individual. We visualise them as the 'CPUL City Clover', a unity of four actions which must happen jointly, but can take on different sizes and shapes (Figure 1).

It is likely that the case studies quoted in this article will soon be overtaken by more rigorous, successful or specialist exemplars, especially if urban agriculture continues to develop at the rate it has over the past decade. If the economic and social infrastructure can be put in place to support it, we could build something far more abundant and significant than that envisaged by a romantic notion of 'growing your own'. Urban agriculture might then answer the fundamental question about our urban future by offering a greater range of experiences while reducing passive consumption.

....

Katrin Bohn and Andre Viljoen are principals at Bohn&Viljoen Architects

....

www.bohnandviljoen.co.uk

Section 2
Food Economies and Their Relationship with a New Social Topography

Using slow money to farm the city

If urban farms are to become more than the latest eco-fad, city farmers will need new economic models to achieve long-term viability. Urban farmers may create lasting businesses if they work to raise consciousness of their place in the global financial system.

....

Derek A Denckla

The financial viability of urban farms is defined by distinct physical limitations: they use very small amounts of space – usually less than an acre – and are cultivated intensively. Urban farms face an uphill struggle to achieve profitability. Today, even small rural farms struggle to stay in business.

Farms outside the city are enterprises expected to sustain themselves through profit and thrift. However, in the developed world, farming has become increasingly dominated by large-scale corporate agribusiness. In this context, the case of small farms in the United States of America (USA) is instructive. Ninety-one percent of farms in the USA are classified as 'small'; having a gross cash farm income of less than $250,000 (€196,000) per annum. About 60 percent of these small farms are very small, generating less than $10,000 (€7,800) per annum. These very small, in some respects non-commercial farms, exist independently of the farm economy because their operators rely heavily on off-farm income.

Overall farm production, however, continues to shift to larger operations, while the number of small commercial farms and their share of sales maintain a long-term decline. In this economic context, urban farms – usually much smaller than even 'small' farms – face unique challenges if they wish to remain viable.

....

Profit over planet

Why are big farms getting bigger, with small farms being squeezed out of the agricultural economy? The answer is clear: access to capital. Large-scale farm businesses can be more efficient, sell more products at a lower cost and achieve more substantial profit margins than their small farm competitors. Investors and creditors provide capital more readily to large farms, expecting as they do higher and more consistent returns on investment. By contrast, investors and creditors perceive small farms to be higher risk, lower reward investments. As a result, small farms often face a cash crunch when seeking investment or credit.

However, large farms – like many large-scale conventional businesses – tend to achieve profits without accounting for negative externalities caused by their agricultural practices. Negative impacts may include soil degradation, fertiliser contamination, excessive use of antibiotics, fossil fuel consumption and poor, low-wage work conditions.

We live in an era of logarithmically enlarging 'hockey stick' returns – positive and negative (Figure 1). The entire financial system is dysfunctional; organised with no meaningful connection to the long-term sustainability of the resources that form its very foundation. Woody Tasch, in his 2008 treatise *Inquiries into the Nature of Slow Money*, puts it very well: 'As it circulates the globe with ever-accelerating speed, money sucks oxygen out of the air, fertility out of the soil and culture out of local community.'

Small farms and urban farms are more likely than large, industrial farms to use sustainable agricultural practices. Yet small farms are largely ignored by the current global financial system even as they are feted by food writers and a growing segment of the public yearning for the pleasures of eating fresh and local produce.

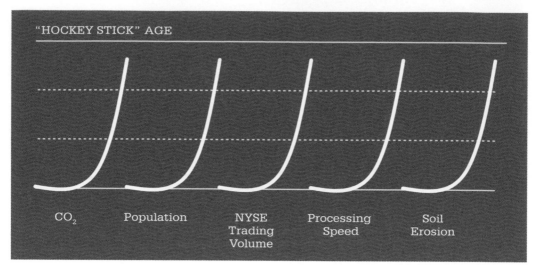

Figure 1 Woody Tasch diagram

Fixing our food systems will inherently address many other pressing, systemic issues: climate change, fossil fuel dependency, health epidemics, hunger and malnutrition. Yet our economic investment models define small farms as a financial problem to be avoided rather than as an ecological solution to be celebrated. By extension, the economic activity of urban farms is so marginal that there are precious few financial services available for them.

....

Think global, act local

Tasch's *Inquiries Into the Nature of Slow Money* presents a vision of social investment focused on placing funds in small and sustainable local agricultural initiatives. These funds would be key to resolving financial issues for small farms and, by extension, relieve major aspects of environmental crisis. Slow Money contrasts with Fast Money, just as Slow Food contrasts with Fast Food.

Investors in small, sustainable farms deviate from the dominant, unsustainable expectation of high profitability and entertain the value of alternative returns such as soil health (planet) and fair trade (people); the basics of a permaculture-inspired approach to production. Slow Money is further defined as investing in real places, in people and in tangible and transparent enterprises close to home. Slowing investment down means developing a more patient rate of return, seeking to build healthy viable enterprises, communities and ecosystems.

Opportunity in crisis

In 2008, the housing boom became a bust in many countries across the globe. The sudden downturn of the economy left a great deal of real estate in an uncertain state of development. At the same time, public interest in urban farms was exploding: urban production captures the imagination of citizens wishing to make the most of difficult circumstances, and to create productive, edible green space across barren, abandoned urban landscapes.

When (and if) the economy improves, will interest in urban farming slip away as more 'profitable' uses for urban space arise? During a similar economic slump in the 1970s, urban agriculture exploded in New York City, USA, giving rise to a national community garden and farm movement. When the economy began to turn around in the late 1980s, however, developers began to pressure the city to release many spaces used by community gardens for private gain. As a result, many community farms and gardens were razed to make way for market rate housing development.

Private investment might support the density and financial viability of urban agriculture, capitalising on sudden economic opportunity and public attention. Raising multiple forms of capital – public and private – would help maximise the chance that urban farms would remain part of the city fabric once the local economy recovers. Lastly, social impact investors would be more willing to accept limited financial returns associated with urban agriculture, if they could be made aware of the social and environmental benefits of urban farming.

In order to remain a fixture of urban space in good times and bad, advocates for urban agriculture have to make the case for seeking and creating several kinds of 'capital' and investment.

Financial and economic capital for urban farms
If urban farms could be run as profitable enterprises, then other business interests would have less traction when competing for use of the same land. However, most urban farms in the United States, in general, and in New York City in particular, are not being run as profitable businesses. Ironically, income from farm produce is not a major source of income for most urban farms.

In addition, urban farms are not usually 'investor-ready' because city farmers do not fully model financial return on investment. However, successful commercial urban farms appear to have one or more of the following five distinct characteristics.

_farm ran a net loss or broke even as a smaller part of a larger related viable business
  (either non-profit or for-profit enterprise);
_farm 'land' (sometimes rooftops) was rent-free or extremely low rent;
_farmer earned most income from non-farm work (so-called 'hobby farm');
_farm made high profit, value-added products from produce, such as hot sauce; or
_farm produced few or single high net profit crop, like leafy greens.

Urban farms may draw on various sources of revenue: sales of produce, sales of compost fertiliser, fees for processing food waste, fees for services (such as educational programmes) and fees for visitors or events. Multiple sources of revenue provide urban farms with less financial risk. However, revenue must be balanced against increased management effort and labour costs for each specialised area of effort. Urban farmers must experiment with many different business models in order to find an optimal operational strategy that leads to long-term success and stable income.

Alternative forms of capital for urban farms
Multiple sources of non-monetary capital may be required to help urban farms reach

viability. Market forces are not just about money; even financial markets respond to social and cultural forces. Luckily, there is significant social, cultural and political momentum around 'Slow Food' and local food. In 2007, for instance, the word *locavore* was chosen by New Oxford American Dictionary as the Word of the Year, defined as 'one who eats food grown locally whenever possible'. Awareness of the need to change a broken food system is growing. The market for organic and local foods continues to experience robust growth, outpacing the conventional foods market.

Successful urban farm enterprises: premium pricing, public education
and government intervention
About one in four American consumers will consistently pay a premium for 'organic' food because they have been educated to feel that these products are better quality and more closely aligned to their environmental values. Urban farm produce will generally cost more to harvest, but may be able to command a premium price along with organic and local foods.

Also, urban farms have some economic efficiencies. For example, intensive growing methods that result in higher yields per acre than conventional farming. Urban farms may also have lower distribution costs, being present inside the market they seek to reach. However, despite these efficiencies, urban farm produce will almost always cost more than conventional produce. Given these realities, how will urban farmers pass their additional costs onto the consumer and realise the true price for their food? A key solution is premium pricing; but, as with investment, higher pricing may only be paid through increased public awareness of social and cultural values of urban agriculture.

Many governments provide incentives, subsidies and protection for rural farms. Urban farms may also need unique support from government, helping urban farms reduce costs of urban produce. Some progressive cities have developed urban agriculture plans, attempting to coordinate government agency action and identify areas for intervention that could benefit urban farms. The following are examples of government interventions that may help improve the bottom line for urban farmers and urban agriculture:

_Special tax incentives tailored to agricultural businesses.

_Reduced business and real estate tax assessments for agricultural uses.

_Reduced land prices and leasing options for city-owned land.

_Expedited and reduced-cost permitting.

_Review and change in laws and regulations such as zoning ordinances, building
 and health codes to encourage and to protect agricultural use and to permit formerly
 prohibited agricultural uses (for example, beekeeping).

_Creating an Ombudsman or Office for Urban Agriculture, to act as a neutral hub
 and to coordinate efforts and information aimed at supporting urban farming.

In conclusion, urban agriculture could play an important role in the community and economic development of cities. However, advocates of urban agriculture should remember that farming is a business. On-going efforts by government, business and activists should be directed to ensure that urban farms may be financially viable in order to provide long-term social, cultural and environmental benefits to cities. Similarly, the non-monetary benefits of urban farms should be carefully explained and demonstrated to consumers, government agents and the new breed of investor who seeks to place funds with enterprises aligned to environmental and social values. With the development of multiple stakeholders, urban farms could weather the shifts in urban economics, politics and land competition that will inevitably arise over time.

....

**Derek Denckla is Chair of Slow Money NYC,
and founder of FarmCityFund.org**

....

www.denckla.com

Future foodscapes

The evolving relationship between cities and the food system suggests that food production systems must become more symbiotically supportive. There are two distinct approaches that can help us make the transition towards a sustainable future.

....

Jan-Willem van der Schans

As cities expand beyond the productive capacity of their hinterlands, the challenge of organising urban food supply in an efficient, resilient, and sustainable manner grows.[1] Two future perspectives offer potential solutions[2]: the 'agri-industrial' and the 'integrated and territorial' food approaches. There is currently much debate within the academic and political worlds as to which perspective is best able to feed the world.

Let us look more specifically at how the two perspectives differ, and what practical solutions they propose (Figure 1). Both approaches consider the typical nature and structure of food production, the organisation of the typical production and distribution chain, and the conventional spatial organisation of production in relation to the urban environment.

....

Structure and nature of food production

In order to become more sustainable, food production systems must move from a linear production model, where inputs are transformed into outputs and (ultimately) waste, to a circular system in which inputs are transformed into outputs that are re-used in the next cycle of production. In the agri-industrial perspective, the closing of loops (water, energy, nutrients) is achieved using technology; in the territorial integrative perspective it occurs naturally.

The agri-industrial perspective is based on a closed system philosophy; for example, a closed greenhouse that harvests surplus solar energy in the summer, stores it underground and re-uses it in the winter. The integrated territorial perspective is rooted in an open system philosophy. Rather than trying to exclude nature, it is invited back into the production system. Natural ecosystems typically perform many functions simultaneously, and are able to cope (within certain limits) with external fluctuations (resilience). An example of this approach can be seen at Hof van Twello, a city-oriented farm close to Deventer, the Netherlands, which combines food production with biodiversity conservation, landscape maintenance and several social initiatives, thus supporting the complete local 'ecosystem'.

It may seem obvious that agriculture in a heavily urbanised environment adopts the agri-industrial perspective of a (semi-) closed food production system. This can be easily integrated within the city fabric, while limiting any negative interaction between food production and the wider environment (soil and air contamination, transfer of pests and diseases). But the process of food production can contribute so much more to the urban experience if it embraces a more territorial integrative perspective and celebrates, rather than suppresses, open interactions with the urban environment.

One example of the agri-industrial perspective is PlantLab, which produces a constant, predictable output of fresh vegetables and herbs by using LED growing lights. Water and nutrients are added as needed, and crops harvested as required. In such a system, natural influences are excluded as much as possible as they could be disruptive to the efficient operation of the system. In contrast, an orchard in the centre of Eva Lanxmeer, Culemborg, the Netherlands, functions as a fruit production site, a public park, a water preservation area and a place of leisure and social enterprise; a great example of the multi-functional territorial integrative perspective.

The organisation of processing and distribution

In understanding the dynamics of urban food supply, it is useful to distinguish between several models of supply chain management and organisation. The territorial integrative food perspective often adopts a supply chain model in which farmers are in direct contact with their customers, and where they bring a range of products to the market depending on the location, the season, and the particular growing context. Many customers are willing to accommodate the limited variety such a system produces, rising to the challenge of cooking with what produce is available, in whatever quantity, (think of vegetable regular box schemes, or a skilled chef who knows how to prepare a red beet in 25 different ways to bring variety to the table).

At the other extreme is the typical agri-industrial supply chain model, where the logic of the conveyer belt processing system is dominant. Farmers are forced to supply standardised inputs and customers are required to accept standardised outputs. It is no coincidence that Henry Ford took the idea of a conveyer belt production system for cars from the pig slaughterhouses of Chicago, which were so efficiently organised that they became the model of industrial production per se.[3]

The original Ford model has given way to a more consumer-friendly version (developed by Toyoda), in which consumers can choose between customisable options, but with original suppliers still producing standardised inputs. The dairy industry is a good example of this type of system: strong, customer-facing brands exist and extensive product development is geared to specific consumer needs, but farmers continue to supply raw milk as a commodity that can be purchased anywhere.

This typical pattern of Toyodistic production has only recently been interrupted, first due to quality requirements imposed by the industry upon primary producers, but more importantly due to the drive for sustainable production models. Original suppliers of raw material, in this case farmers producing milk, vegetables or meat, now need to clearly differentiate themselves and their products. Farmers who achieve outstanding levels of quality or sustainability contribute to the brand value of the processor, and become strategic partners to be nurtured rather than raw material suppliers to be exploited.

This post-Toyodistic chain model - where both customers and suppliers are unique – is still developing, but already we see major players experimenting with its details, and it is expected that farmers who adopt this model will - ultimately - benefit. For example, when supplying milk for the Campina brand, farmers are invited to comply with certain criteria. For example, cows should be at pasture in the meadows for a certain period each year, with farmers compensated for any extra costs incurred. This system demonstrates some link between customer and producer in an industrial context, even if it is not the direct one-to-one link outlined in the integrated territorial model.

Another example is Willem and Drees, a fresh vegetables and fruits wholesaler that commits itself to a 40-kilometre regional supply chain, but in the meantime sells its produce in national supermarket chains. Thus it combines the efficiency of the conventional retail system with the quality of the alternative food system. Another example is the restaurant chain La Place. It only serves meals that are prepared from fresh

RIVAL PRODUCTION CONCEPTS

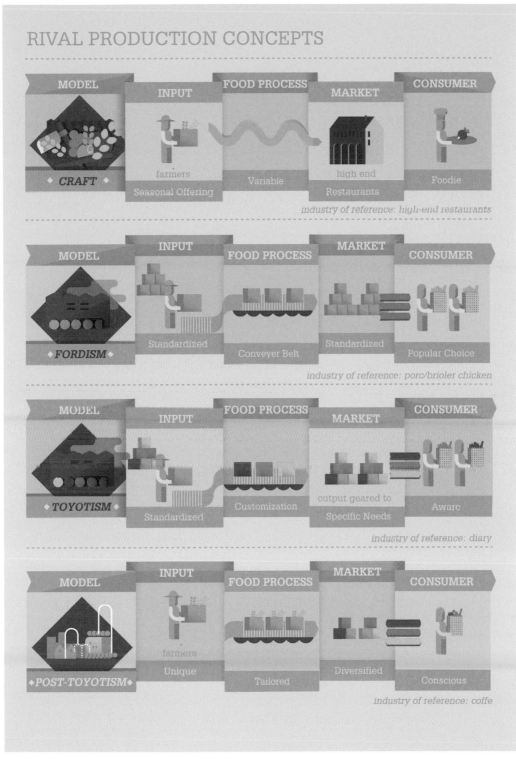

Figure 1 Rival Production Concepts

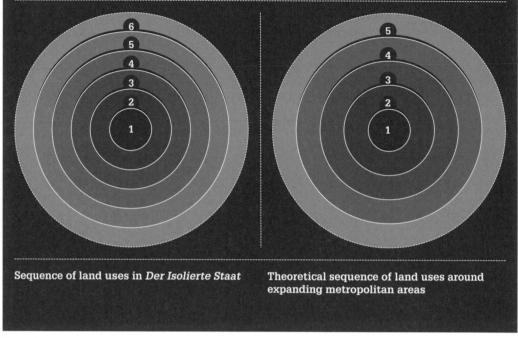

1 market gardening & fresh milk
2 firewood & lumber
3 intensive crop farming (grazing & root crops)
4 crop farming (with fallow and pasture)
5 three-field rotation
6 grazing

1 urban farming
2 vacant grazing (temporary)
3 field crop & grazing (transition)
4 dairying & field crop
5 specialized feed-grain livestock

Sequence of land uses in *Der Isolierte Staat*

Theoretical sequence of land uses around expanding metropolitan areas

Figure 2 Spatial organisation of the production

ingredients on the premises; increasingly these ingredients come from farmers located close to the restaurants (slow food, but served fast).

These models of supply chain organisation and network analysis are relevant because they demonstrate that feeding cities is a complex and dynamic challenge; one which cannot be met by encouraging conventional approaches to become more sustainable, or by stimulating alternative approaches to scale up and become more efficient. Both strategies must be pursued; the critical issue will be interaction between the two.

....

Spatial organisation of production (Figure 2)

In the agri-industrial perspective, food production and other land uses such as natural spaces, recreation, urban living and industry are spatially separated and clustered in specialised zones. This happens in order to reduce the potential impact of negative interaction between different uses and to allow for the optimal use of land within a specific zone. Before industrialisation, food production was spatially organised in such a way that highly-valued perishable crops and dairy products would be located in and around cities[4], whereas staple crops and extensive beef production requiring pasture for grazing were located further away from the city (livestock would walk to the city where it would be fattened and slaughtered).

As industrialisation progressed, land uses further away from the city intensified, and increasing mechanisation allowed for the scaling up of production, harvesting, processing and transportation. As cities expanded, urban and peri-urban farmers wishing to capitalise on increases in land values stopped investing in their farms, with the result that agricultural land use patterns in and around expanding cities became extensive and temporary.[5] Such patterns of land use lead to the segregation of food production and urban dwelling systems.

Due to the recent economically-sparked urban development crisis, however, open spaces in and around cities are no longer being quickly developed. City-orientated farmers are being invited back to the land to grow food, perhaps temporarily, but always as a deliberate strategy to smooth the transition from expansion to equilibrium. One example is the Polder Schieveen above Rotterdam, which was acquired by the City of Rotterdam for transformation into an industrial zone and new nature reserve. But the plan was postponed, and it became evident that the polder's biodiversity increased when the bought-out farmers began to use the land more extensively, having only one-year leases. Farmers invited back to the land in this way are required to respect biodiversity and to orientate food production towards city dwellers. These moves follow the integrated and territorial perspective, where food production is aimed at the local market, adapted to the local context and integrated with other functions of the landscape, such as biodiversity preservation, recreation and education.

....

Conclusions

To conclude, we return briefly to the debate between agri-industrial advocates and integrated territorial proponents: which of the two perspectives will be able to feed a growing global and increasingly urban population (Figure 3)? The debate has been framed in such a way that the two perspectives are in competition rather than being complementary: in fact, it is entirely possible that a mix of agri-industrial and territorial integrated food production will emerge.

Indeed, it is interesting to note that some of the most remarkable initiatives today make use of components from both the agri-industrial and the territorial integrated perspectives. For example greenhouse company Bijo grows its vegetables according to organic standards (soil-based), but also reduces its CO_2 emissions by harvesting solar energy in summer, storing it in underground aquifers and using it in winter (the closed greenhouse concept, as discussed earlier).

This suggests an innovative vision of agri-food production in which different perspectives contribute to an increasingly sustainable urban food supply: one perspective bringing in the introduction of new urban consumer trends, and the other bringing about efficiency in

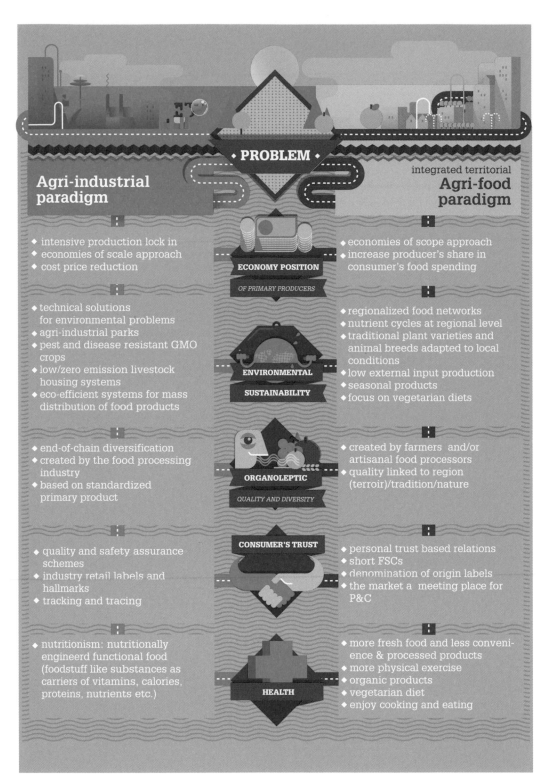

PROBLEM

Agri-industrial paradigm

integrated territorial
Agri-food paradigm

ECONOMY POSITION
OF PRIMARY PRODUCERS

- intensive production lock in
- economies of scale approach
- cost price reduction

- economies of scope approach
- increase producer's share in consumer's food spending

ENVIRONMENTAL SUSTAINABILITY

- technical solutions for environmental problems
- agri-industrial parks
- pest and disease resistant GMO crops
- low/zero emission livestock housing systems
- eco-efficient systems for mass distribution of food products

- regionalized food networks
- nutrient cycles at regional level
- traditional plant varieties and animal breeds adapted to local conditions
- low external input production
- seasonal products
- focus on vegetarian diets

ORGANOLEPTIC
QUALITY AND DIVERSITY

- end-of-chain diversification
- created by the food processing industry
- based on standardized primary product

- created by farmers and/or artisanal food processors
- quality linked to region (terroir)/tradition/nature

CONSUMER'S TRUST

- quality and safety assurance schemes
- industry retail labels and hallmarks
- tracking and tracing

- personal trust based relations
- short FSCs
- denomination of origin labels
- the market a meeting place for P&C

HEALTH

- nutritionism: nutritionally engineerd functional food (foodstuff like substances as carriers of vitamins, calories, proteins, nutrients etc.)

- more fresh food and less convenience & processed products
- more physical exercise
- organic products
- vegetarian diet
- enjoy cooking and eating

Figure 3 Food Geographies

production, processing and distribution, and creating a link with an international trading system that is inclusive, equitable, and cosmopolitan. Welcome to the metropolitan foodscape of the 21st century!

....

Jan-Willem van der Schans is a researcher in urban food supply, markets and supply chains at the Agricultural Economics Research Institute and the Rural Sociology Group, Wageningen University

....

www.wageningenur.nl

Local food, fresh and fair

Fair Food Network's Double Up Food Bucks (DUFB) programme's aim is to increase the economic viability of urban farmers, improve the local economy and address the need of low-income urban residents for healthy, fresh food.

....

Oran B Hesterman Ph.D.

Fair Food Network's Double Up Food Bucks (DUFB) in Michigan, USA, is a simple and effective idea (Picture 1). When recipients of federal Supplemental Nutrition Assistance Programme benefits (SNAP, formerly known as food stamps) shop at participating farmers' markets, the amount of money that they spend using their SNAP card is matched with tokens worth up to $20 per visit. With these tokens they can purchase any Michigan-grown produce at the market. This helps to keep the flow of resources in the community and supports the economic productivity and sustainability of local farms.

Based on the vision and mission of Fair Food Network (FFN), an organisation dedicated to building a just and sustainable food system, the concept of a 'double value' coupon project for recipients of federal food assistance, valid at farmers' markets, seemed like an important first step in providing greater access to wholesome, fresh food for inner city residents.

I first saw this idea put into practice at a farmers' market in Takoma Park, Maryland, in 2007 when I was a programme director at the W. K. Kellogg Foundation, which had given a small grant to a healthy food incentive progamme at this market. Several other outlets were also starting to emerge with this idea, many sponsored by non-profit organisations such as Wholesome Wave in Connecticut and marketumbrella.org in New Orleans.

Because the availability of healthy food is such a challenge in Detroit, just a one hour drive from the FFN's headquarters, it seemed a natural place to experiment with this type of incentive programme. Double Up Food Bucks started in 2009 as a pilot project at Detroit's Eastern Market and four other farmers' markets in the city. It expanded to 54 markets by 2011 and in 2012 was available at more than 100 sites, including farmers' markets, farm stands, and mobile produce trucks. It reaches tens of thousands of Michigan residents and benefits hundreds of local farmers.

DUFB creates an economic multiplier in the local economy, increasing the number of new shoppers and producers who support each other. In the USA, more than 46 million people receive $72 billion in federal SNAP benefits.[1] If SNAP recipients spent their food assistance dollars at farmers' markets at the same rate as the general public spends money, they would create a flow of over $130 million to local farmers and food systems. Taking into account the dramatic rise in the number of farmers' markets nationally, a 450 per cent increase since the United States Department of Agriculture (USDA) officially started tracking farmers' markets in 1994, there is great potential to use the innovative DUFB programme as a catalyst for transformation in our inner cities.[2]

The programme has also had a profound effect on growers who sell at the market (Picture 2). Fifth-generation farmer Case Visser, a vendor at the Fulton Street Farmers Market in Grand Rapids, Michigan states: 'I'm passionate about Double Up Food Bucks because I have seen it change people's lives. We ended up getting a lot of business from it … It's a great thing to be involved in. Our farm is proud to support it.'
....

The need: overcoming food deserts
A USDA-led study on the incidence of food deserts defines them as 'areas with limited access to affordable and nutritious food, particularly such an area composed of

Picture 1 Vegetables and DUFB sign (top left)
Picture 2 Cash register with DUFB tokens (top right)
Picture 3 Marlyn Minus & Mel Holtz at Eastern Market (bottom right)
Picture 4 Efigenia Rojas, Altonens Orchards (bottom left)

predominantly lower-income neighbourhoods and communities.'[3] Substantial areas of many urban centres fit this description: in Detroit, more than half a million residents live in neighbourhoods where they must travel twice as far to reach a grocery store as a convenience store, gas station or liquor store, and where healthy, fresh food is difficult to find. As a result, they are frequently compelled to purchase low-quality, highly-processed products, often at higher prices than in the suburbs.[4]

Marlyn Minus, with her nine children in tow, shops at Detroit Eastern Market with her DUFB tokens: 'With Double Up Food Bucks I can try different fruits and vegetables and feed more healthy food to my children than I ever could before. My children can't wait to get home and taste these apples and strawberries.' Marlyn buys delicious fresh fruit from Mel Holtz, farmer at the Holtz Family Farm in Ida, Michigan, 60 miles from downtown Detroit. Mel and his family have been selling their crops at the market since 1968. They are appreciative of the DUFB programme, which allows them to expand their already diverse offerings of produce at the market as well as increase their income (Picture 3).[5]

Providing greater access to local farmers' affordable, fresh produce in urban farmers' markets addresses the diet-related health issues that are prevalent in under-served communities. Lack of access to healthy food, particularly fresh fruits and vegetables,

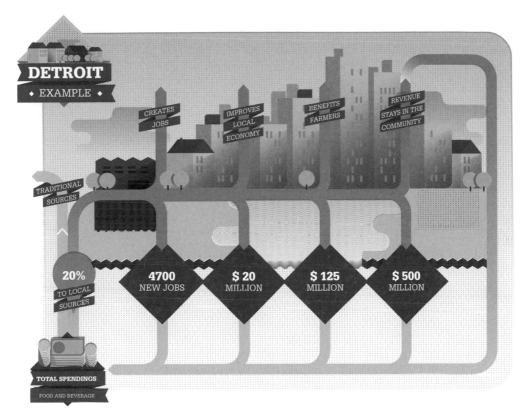

DETROIT
• EXAMPLE •

CREATES JOBS

IMPROVES LOCAL ECONOMY

BENEFITS FARMERS

REVENUE STAYS IN THE COMMUNITY

TRADITIONAL SOURCES

20% TO LOCAL SOURCES

| 4700 NEW JOBS | $ 20 MILLION | $ 125 MILLION | $ 500 MILLION |

TOTAL SPENDINGS
FOOD AND BEVERAGE

Figure 1 Supporting DUFB and local food enterprises: the example of Detroit

is linked to the growing epidemic of diet-related chronic diseases such as diabetes and heart disease. Again, Detroit is an example of what is happening nationwide wherever healthy, fresh produce is not readily available: over 70 per cent of Detroit's adults[6] and close to 40 per cent of its youth[7] are overweight or obese. Rates of diabetes and heart disease are higher than state and national averages.[8] Making local farmers' produce available to these inner city residents, such as Marlyn Minus (Picture 4), has the potential to immediately shift eating patterns and improve health outcomes, particularly for children.

Supporting DUFB and local food enterprises could significantly benefit farmers, improve local economies, and create jobs. Using Detroit as an example, if we divert 20 per cent of food and beverage spending in Detroit toward local sources, we could increase the city's annual output by nearly half a billion dollars, add 4,700 new jobs, pay $125 million more in earnings, and provide the city with $20 million in added business taxes (Figure 1).[9]

Drawing on the federal funds available in the Detroit metro area via the SNAP programme, DUFB is contributing to localising our food economy: spent locally at DUFB sites, these funds go directly into the pockets of regional farmers, producers, and entrepreneurs. In this way, the revenue stays in the community and recirculates, stoking the fires of

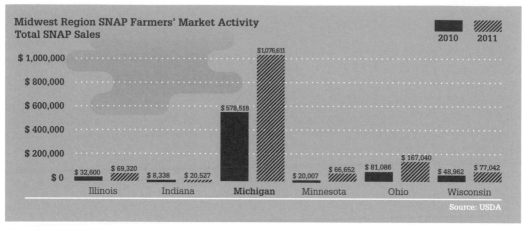

Figure 2 Total SNAP Sales

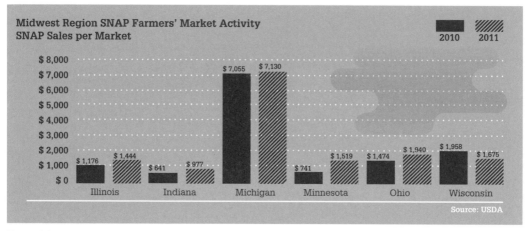

Figure 3 SNAP Sales per Market

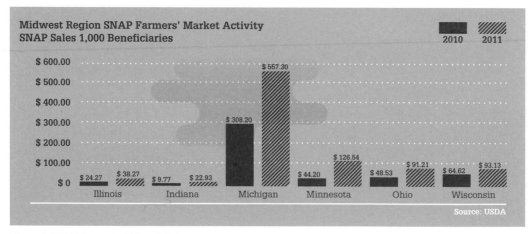

Figure 4 SNAP Sales per 1,000 Beneficiaries

Picture 5 Billboard

commerce and creating jobs in the urban and peri-urban areas, jobs that generate additional economic activity.

DUFB is attracting low-income shoppers to urban farmers' markets that were previously visited by a more affluent group of shoppers. We believe that in the long run this rebalancing of attraction and access will see farmers' markets evolving: becoming lively public spaces that serve as gathering places for people from a variety of ethnic backgrounds, races, and classes.

....

A new customer base

In 2011, SNAP recipients made over 40,000 visits to participating farmers' markets, and SNAP and DUFB sales in those markets reached more than $1.3 million. Almost a third of the DUFB shoppers used their benefits at a farmers' market for the first time ever, creating a new customer base for local farmers. Evaluation results further show a 190 per cent increase in SNAP purchases at participating markets since our programme began. Eighty percent of farmers report selling more fresh fruits and/or vegetables and making more money, and more than three-quarters of the vendors see new clients at their stalls.[10] As of July 31, 2012, combined DUFB and SNAP use at Michigan farmers' markets has already exceeded last year's results by 36 per cent.

The charts opposite (Figures 2–4) illustrate how much greater SNAP redemptions were at Michigan farmers' markets than at those in the other Midwestern states during 2011: there is no doubt that the DUFB programme contributed to these staggering differences.

....

Scaling up the model

The success of the DUFB programme at Michigan farmers' markets has led to the development of two innovative projects that will further expand urban and peri-urban farmers' access to the SNAP market. Fair Food Network has received permission from the USDA to be the first to bring a SNAP incentive programme into three grocery stores, all located in the city of Detroit, simultaneously preventing leakage of urban grocery dollars to suburban retail stores, and meeting inner-city demand for fresh produce. In addition, FFN's Detroit Grocery Incubator provides support to aspiring grocery entrepreneurs while creating business opportunities for local farms, food processors, distribution networks, and retailers.

Currently, DUFB draws on a reservoir of funds raised from over 40 community and private foundations and corporations to match SNAP purchases. As our future agriculture and food policy is created with the reauthorisation of the Farm Bill, there is an opportunity to access public funding for this practical approach to improving agricultural development and access to healthy food (Picture 5).

In a W.K. Kellogg Foundation nationwide poll, 75 percent of people polled support a national programme to double the value of SNAP benefits when used at farmers' markets.[11] In a move that mirrors constituents' feelings, both the Senate and House Agriculture Committees, together with the full Senate, voted in summer 2012 to include support for incentive-type programmes in their versions of the Farm Bill, indicating bi-partisan support for implementations of healthy food incentive programmes nationwide. In the summary of the Senate Committee's Agriculture Reform, Food and Jobs Act 2012, DUFB is even mentioned by name as a replicable model. It's a programme that brings together urban and rural producers and consumers for resilient economic growth, enabling legislators from both sides of the aisle and from diverse geographic locations to have a stake in its passage.

With the vast amount of money being provided by the government in food assistance, a huge opportunity exists to use that money wisely to support our local farmers, and to enable low-income families to eat more healthily. If the incentive measure passes, the USDA will be in a position to provide funds for programmes similar to DUFB across the country, bringing new vitality and energy to our urban centres, and empowering the public and private sector to support and reinforce each other's work, creating a synergistic relationship that multiplies the effectiveness of the programme.

Double Up Food Bucks[12] continues to prove that a small incentive can result in broader markets and increased earnings for farmers in urban areas. DUFB is a replicable, scalable model that could potentially leverage billions of dollars in federal funds allocated to federal food assistance to spur local economic activity, particularly for small and mid-sized farmers.

....

Oran B Hesterman, Ph.D. is President
and CEO, Fair Food Network

....

www.fairfoodnetwork.org

Possibilities and pitfalls: urban food security

FoodShare Toronto is increasing access to fresh produce by supporting community-run produce markets across the city. It is rebalancing the political and economic dynamics affecting urban food security and food distribution, and transforming the urban and economic environment through food.

....

Jennifer Sumner, JJ McMurtry and Michael Classens

FoodShare Toronto is among Canada's largest non-profit community food advocacy and programme providers. Launched in the autumn of 1985, it had a three-month mandate to coordinate the burgeoning food bank system in the city. FoodShare quickly realised, however, that food banks were only temporary solutions to hunger, and did nothing to address the structural causes of food insecurity. So it sought continued public funding to, among other things, design programmes to encourage low-income groups to start their own co-operative grocery stores, food-buying clubs and gardens.

By 1992, FoodShare began organising 'food stores' in the lobbies of buildings belonging to Canada's largest public housing provider, the Metro Toronto Housing Authority, in order to increase tenants' accessibility to fresh produce. It purchased the produce from local farmers through the Ontario Food Terminal, the main produce distribution centre for Toronto, and delivered it to low-income communities across the city.

The project's key aim was the rebalancing of the political and economic dynamics affecting food security and food distribution in the city. Within a few years, FoodShare had transformed a short-term mandate into a multifaceted community-based agency – an advocacy organisation, a non-profit food distribution service, and a coordinator of food provisioning services with the capacity and resources to bring its demands to both the provincial and federal governments. Now a multi-million-dollar organisation, FoodShare represents a key presence in the alternative food politics of Toronto.

One of FoodShare's recent projects is the Good Food Market (GFM) programme. This supports the establishment of community-run fresh produce markets by acting as a liaison between alternative and conventional wholesale distribution systems and residents within low-income and marginalised communities across Toronto.

The development of the GFM programme can be traced to its Metro Toronto Housing Authority 'food store' initiative of the early 1990s. Understanding the increasingly spatial dimension of food insecurity in the city, while defining the issue as part of a broader socio-economic problem (housing and income), FoodShare sought an explicitly place-based social strategy for increasing food security.

To this end, the GFM programme joined a constellation of other services aligned in Toronto's 'priority neighbourhoods'. A landmark study by United Way Toronto in 2004 demonstrated that the overall income gap in Toronto was widening, and that poverty had worsened in existing low-income neighbourhoods over the past 20 years. Since the publication of the report, non-profit service providers and the municipal government have joined forces to provide a range of services to Toronto's most marginalised neighbourhoods. The GFM programme is therefore no longer confined to the lobbies of public housing units, but has expanded operations to 16 communities within the Greater Toronto Area (GTA), most of which are identified as priority neighbourhoods, making use of a variety of neighbourhood spaces, including community centres and the lobbies of other community-service agencies.

The concept of the GFM programme is simple: FoodShare is able to procure relatively inexpensive fresh produce through bulk purchasing from both the Ontario Food Terminal and farmers in the region. Host residents are responsible for on-the-ground organisation of the markets within their communities. These organisers make weekly orders for produce, based on typical volume of sales, resident requests, and availability, and FoodShare delivers the order to the host market. Market organisers buy the produce from FoodShare at cost, a price that does not include, for example, the cost of delivery. By only charging for the cost of the food, FoodShare is indirectly subsidising the programme and ensuring that the produce sold at the markets remains as inexpensive as possible. FoodShare also provides training and networking opportunities for resident organisers, as well as a flexible support regime determined by the needs of the particular community.

In addition to increasing access to inexpensive, fresh produce, the GFM programme also attempts to build place and strengthen community, reflecting FoodShare's broader understanding of the socio-spatial elements of hunger and food insecurity. The neighbourhoods that host GFMs tend to be under-serviced by conventional food distribution channels (grocery stores), meaning that people have to travel further for their food. At the same time, people in those neighbourhoods tend to have less time and money to travel the distances required of them. GFMs target lower-income and marginalised communities, and illustrate FoodShare's understanding of the related nature of place and socio-economic marginalisation.

But the politics of the GFMs go beyond the particular socio-spatial strategy developed for the distribution of affordable food to Toronto's 'food deserts'. By procuring much of the food distributed at the GFMs from local farmers, the organisation is also attempting to forge an alternative food network, disentangled from the globalised and overly-commoditized conventional food system, while re-creating more localised producer-consumer linkages in the GTA's foodscape. In rejecting, and seeking to circumvent, the conventional food system, the GFM programme takes on the double task of re-shaping both the demand side and the supply side of a more just and effective local food system.

A recent study highlighted some possibilities and pitfalls for this kind of food-based urban development.[1] In terms of possibilities, the study revealed that the GFM programme does a better job of offering culturally appropriate and affordable food than FoodShare's other programmes. It also promotes community by creating public spaces within which neighbours gather to socialise. In other words, the GFM programme addresses issues of both food deserts and 'community space deserts', although its potential to support the vibrancy of public spaces within the community is under-realised. GFMs also promote the development of community economic capacity and knowledge.

A key benefit of the markets was their ability to create linkages between service providers in particular neighbourhoods. Market customers were found to be dedicated to attending the market and discerning when it came to appreciating the higher quality and lower price of GFM produce. Market volunteers took pride in their role in making the GFM available within their communities and were motivated by the challenge of making healthy and affordable food accessible. Some of the larger markets have integrated specialised tasks, such as accounting and marketing, into their organisation's existing administrative departments, which leverages existing internal capacities while taking pressure off market volunteers (although not all of the markets have access to this level of expertise). Most market volunteers are also motivated to increase the number of people attending the market on a weekly basis.

In terms of pitfalls, the study showed that market coordinators (many of whom are volunteers) must commit a significant amount of time to organising the markets, and need a wide array of skillsets including fiscal management and accounting, communication and marketing abilities, fundraising savvy, and volunteer management skills. In addition, FoodShare staff are, at times, doing too much of the week-to-week organisation of individual markets, which monopolises their time and squanders the opportunities to build local capacity for community organising.

Yet another pitfall involves the logistics of productively using left-over produce. In many cases, this produce is simply given away, creating revenue loss and generally meaning that those markets operate at a weekly loss. In a related logistical pitfall, the weekly produce delivery takes a significant amount of FoodShare's time and resources.

Another challenge involves easing the tensions inherent in social business. On the one hand, FoodShare wants to operate the GFM programme as a social enterprise, and as a means of creating revenue (however meagre) for either the individual markets, FoodShare, or both. On the other hand, FoodShare also wants to facilitate access to low-cost and easily accessible produce for low-income and marginalised populations. These tensions can create long-standing problems for social-purpose organisations.

In spite of these issues, a number of positive considerations arise from this study. First, since the GFMs are a key interface through which FoodShare connects with the broader public, they could be considered ambassadors for FoodShare's broader social mandate. In practical terms, the GFM programme becomes a means of broader volunteer recruitment, a vehicle through which to share ideas about food issues, and a way of spreading information about other FoodShare programmes. Additionally, the GFM programme could be re-framed as a permanent weekly meeting place for those looking to engage more substantively with contemporary food issues.

Secondly, the GFMs could better link and leverage within their own host organisations, as well as with existing community programmes, services and infrastructures, especially in terms of their broader social change goals. If the GFMs, for example, were to link their activities more explicitly with the co-operative food distributers and marketers in Toronto, then they might improve both the cost of their goods as well as the variety of goods available.

Many of the market visitors and volunteers understand the very act of attending the markets as a distinctly political one. They see their various contributions to the GFMs as an explicit attempt to respond to the deficiencies and injustices of the contemporary food system within an urban context and as a means of working towards a more just and sustainable food system. Bringing these nascent feelings together organisationally, in a local urban setting, has significant potential to empower these communities.

On the one hand, this is cause for celebration. Simply by virtue of being at the market, participants feel that they are actively involved in a political project. At the same time, residents are building alternative social infrastructures within their communities, creating meeting spaces, fostering friendships, strengthening networks and enriching place. They are fundamentally transforming their urban and economic environment through food.

Such enthusiasm, dedication and political commitment should be further leveraged, both within the GFM communities and beyond, toward other activities designed to promote more just, food-based urban development. For example, with a municipal election less than two years away, FoodShare has an opportunity to engage, via the GFM programme, in a policy and programming conversation as a way to bring food issues to the forefront of the campaign agenda. Linking up with other food-related programmes across the city could create an opportunity to mobilise a vast electorate primed to demand, for example, an end to food deserts in the city.

On the other hand, there is good reason to be careful of too hastily celebrating the potential of the GFM programme to successfully transform either the contemporary food system, or the low-income neighbourhoods in which the markets operate. On this front, questions abound. Is the GFM programme simply instilling a kind of limited consumer activism? How is it addressing the broader structural issues that result in an unjust food system in the first place? Are struggling communities being further marginalised by having to take on the task of basic food provision for their residents? Is it deflecting attention from governments unwilling to address issues of poverty?

In the deeply neoliberal environment of North America, non-market solutions to problems (many of which are caused by fundamental market failures) have little chance of support from any level of government. We know that poverty in local communities cannot be simply solved by action in one area such as food provision, however important, as the experience of food banks across Canada has shown. As a result, food and poverty activists are increasingly linking these struggles in a more holistic understanding of their actions and the problem itself (for example, the historical change of focus within the mission of the Daily Bread Food Bank from hunger to poverty).

In short, the GFM programme in Toronto demonstrates the complexity of re-shaping the conventional food system, while shedding light on the limits and possibilities of using food as a tool for urban development. Battling food insecurity and repairing fractured communities through place-making present steep challenges, but must remain part of the urban development agenda in Toronto. While regressive austerity politics threaten to further erode already-anaemic structures of social, cultural and environmental sustainability, the case of the GFMs gives us reason to be cautiously optimistic about the future our cities and our food system.

....

Jennifer Sumner teaches in the Adult Education
and Community Development Program at
OISE/University of Toronto, JJ McMurtry is
Program Director of the Graduate Program in
Social and Political Thought at York University,
and Michael Classens is a PhD Candidate in
the Faculty of Environmental Studies
at York University

Section 3
Urban Society; Citizens, Artists and Activists

Adopt, accept, appreciate

Local communities are transforming public spaces into socially driven, edible urban foodscapes producing organically grown fruit, herbs, flowers and vegetables. But convincing decision makers of the generative power within such bottom-up movements is a complex and lengthy process.

....

Debra Solomon & Mariska van den Berg

URBANIAHOEVE, Social Design Lab for Urban Agriculture, was established in the Netherlands in 2010. Its contextual framework lies in spatial planning and public space; its team works to produce food system infrastructure; creating park-like, productive ecosystems, often within existing ornamental plantings. It explores ways in which collectively organised ecological social systems function within neighbourhoods. In Dutch, URBANIAHOEVE means 'the city (as a) farmyard', suggesting that the urban, built environment is one place where we might 'get ourselves back to the garden'.

URBANIAHOEVE creates '*foodscapes*'; urban landscapes that connect all elements of food-related urban ecosystems, from urban green spaces, open-air kitchens and markets to groups of neighbours, high school biology students and their teachers, and social gardening clubs. Creating these foodscapes requires diverse forms of bottom-up activation of existing social structures at the neighbourhood level.

Within the context of art, URBANIAHOEVE's work is considered to be critical spatial practice. Within the context of architecture and urban planning, it demonstrates the empirical application of an holistic approach to the human-city-nature complex. This involves a qualitative reconsideration of the city's public space and its uses, rather than the objective application of statistical and quantitative inquiry.

....

Foodscape Schilderswijk

From 2010 onwards, in close collaboration with the art and architecture centre Stroom Den Haag, the URBANIAHOEVE team has worked on *Foodscape Schilderswijk*, creating a continuous productive landscape in the existing green infrastructure, built with the local community in The Hague. *Foodscape Schilderswijk* is a series of public space orchards, created and maintained by a diverse range of local groups. The harvest from these spaces (fruit, berries, soft fruit, artichokes, rhubarb, perennial herbs and flowers) is publicly available and can be freely picked. The less tangible, but equally important harvest of this project – increased activity across public spaces, increased social cohesion and community solidarity, and a radical and steady increase in biodiversity and conviviality – is also free for the community to enjoy.

'Realistic utopianism without irony' is one of the slogans emblazoned on the URBANIAHOEVE *Foodscape Schilderswijk* project posters. This tongue-in-cheek expression underscores the intention of creating edible landscapes that are practical examples of the urban agriculture we desire: green, social, communal, spatial, and public. We do not question if this process works, we experiment with how it works, with every intention of creating a thriving and lasting scenario.

The Hague's Schilderswijk was designed in a 1980s wave of Dutch urban renewal, the existing public greens are purely decorative; out of reach beyond fences and landscaped barriers. For urban agriculture to be successful in the Schilderswijk within this spatial context, it must positively impact resilience at ecological, social, and nutritional levels.

Our team's experience has taught us that growing nutritional food crops, along with the social landscape that can support them, is far more valuable to a neighbourhood than the production and sale of 'consumer grade' food items such as organic produce.

The Foodscape Schilderswijk community possesses neither the means nor the ambition to buy organic food. In these neighbourhoods, awareness of the value of locally grown fruit and vegetables, of a healthy natural environment and a healthy relationship with one's neighbours, will come readily when that product is free for the taking, both in terms of consumption and participation.

An important element that contributes to the success of *Foodscape Schilderswijk* is our effective working relationship with the Parks and Greens Department of the Hague municipality (Groen Beheer). In future, we will strengthen this relationship by producing toolkits for work and planting packages, encouraging further collaboration between organisations. We support each other with plant material, labour and technical knowledge, and Groen Beheer proved to be a valuable ally when sceptical bureaucrats needed convincing during the early stages of *Foodscape Schilderswijk*'s development.

Groen Beheer provides URBANIAHOEVE's teams with local, strategic advocacy. Due to a mutually positive experience, an informal relationship is maintained that allows us to continue to develop project locations according to need. Groen Beheer makes suggestions regarding plant engineering, and facilitates works requiring machinery or technical support. After two years of collaboration, each participant in the partnership is well-acquainted with the municipality's ambitions and timetables for the Schilderswijk, just as Groen Beheer is familiar with *Foodscape Schilderswijk*'s ambitions and 'landscape language'.

Needless to say, the road from autonomous public space art project to respectable municipal stakeholder is arduous. The positive working relationship between URBANIAHOEVE and the municipality has taken time and hard work to develop. Three years into *Foodscape Schilderswijk*, we are still evolving the common vocabulary necessary to bridge the cultural and professional gaps which, if not overcome, could potentially derail the vision.

....

Public Reaction
Not all Schilderswijk neighbours have reacted positively to the foodscapes project. A vocal minority greets each new development with a negative attitude, choosing to reject the possibility that a participatory public space landscape could have any positive impact on civic behaviour. Yet it can and does: along the south-west facing wall of the project's Hanneman Hoek, adjacent to a sanctioned dog-poop zone, mothers and children from the local elementary school planted a collection of pear trees flanked with currants, abundant (and somewhat over-productive) rhubarb, and artichokes. The local high school biology class also planted aromatic plants to overpower the smell of the nearby poop along the dividing fence.

In just one year, the Hanneman Hoek has flourished and has produced a significant, albeit rhubarb-rich, harvest for the neighbourhood. The doubters have finally been partially convinced: the area has seen increasing numbers of ad hoc visits, and neighbours who once vocally eschewed the edible landscape now openly agree that the project is a success. Now, the dissenters focus their venom on our rhubarb recipes. And although each emerging location is met with scepticism, within one year of completion each Foodscape Schilderswijk site has been adopted, accepted and appreciated.

....

Small-scale Infrastructure

The bubble of artist autonomy in the early 2000s was a strong driver for culturally-driven urban agriculture and urban regeneration in the Netherlands. But this bubble dramatically burst in 2011, when the Dutch minority cabinet announced draconian funding cuts. Along with many other bottom-up infrastructure producers in this era of partially dismantled government, Urbaniahoeve now operates in an uncertain and precarious future.

Our teams are involved in implementing radical notions of urban agriculture. Because the alternatives presented in URBANIAHOEVE visions are formulated outside of existing professional institutions, these new futures are often regarded with distrust. Complex and lengthy negotiation is the only modus operandi available for informing and convincing decision makers. Alternative visions tend to express a desire for democratic processes to govern the development and management of our cities' public and common spaces. Decision making parties in the field frequently fail to recognise the generative power within bottom-up movements, and their potential for valuable innovation. Citizens who formulate visions for their living environments are acting upon their own needs and desires, and have proven both creative and highly effective in the development of the necessary strategies to realise their ideas.

In the case of the URBANIAHOEVE *foodscapes*, neighbours and local institutions are approached informally. Everyone is able to get involved, based upon mutual interest and shared values. This approach results in new social connections that, over time, become sufficiently robust to carry the project forward. It also embeds a renewed sense of belonging within the neighbourhood, a feeling of being 'at home' and, at the same time, connected to wider urban processes. Regrettably, this feeling is frequently absent in the neighbourhoods in which we work.

Within the URBANIAHOEVE team, we recognise our own need to intervene in the development of our urban environment, and to participate in the creation of the city. With this in mind, we develop and test new processes that support involvement and commitment. After almost three years of working on *foodscapes*, we feel that our work, and that of similar initiatives both in the Netherlands and abroad, provides valuable models for social and democratic innovation. When we speak of 'event practice' or 'critical spatial practice', we use the term practice not in opposition to theory, but in the sense of action research. At each *foodscape* location we begin work from scratch, with a clear vision carried out through an open process of incremental development, participation and shared decision making.

Urbaniahoeve's vision of urban public spaces as *foodscapes* is rooted in the notion of a productive, socio-natural city. In times of austerity, when true socio-environmental costs remain hidden, an urban agriculture event/critical spatial practice provides a platform for the development of new forms of long-term support frameworks. This process incorporates a deep dialectical foundation; it is not exclusively a producer of urban food

Picture 1 Foodscape Schilderswijk participants plant polyculture orchard in the public space (top)
Picture 2 Announcing the new planting to the neighbourhood (middle left)
Picture 3 Foodscape multi-layer orchard polyculture after 18 months is completely self-sustaining (middle right)
Picture 4 Foodscape Schilderswijk participants plant nectar route (bottom)

infrastructure, but also a generator of new notions of socio-environmental relationships, horizontally produced urban infrastructure, and community innovation.

....

Debra Solomon and Mariska van den Berg
work with Urbaniahoeve

....

www.urbaniahoeve.nl

Community Food: the Role of Artists

Artists can help to bridge gaps within communities and between stakeholders, but can they also demonstrate impact on strategy or policymaking?

....

Alex Wilde and Annechien Meier

Artists Alex Wilde from Scotland, UK, and Annechien Meier from the Netherlands have been working together on the collaborative project *A Growing Exchange* since February 2011. The project explores the role of the artist in projects related to food, community growing and urban agriculture in The Hague and Glasgow.

There is a groundswell of interest in urban agriculture across a range of disciplines, and artists are no exception; they have been exploring key issues in this field for the past ten years, working with a variety of spaces and communities. There's much to explore: how much responsibility should artists have in these initiatives? Should artists have a role in addressing social and economic challenges? Speaking for ourselves, we are still working on our responses, although one thing is clear. In our experience, the growing interest in urban agriculture is currently far from mainstream. There are many communities who are not part of the debate, and whose choices and experiences in relation to food remain limited.

In Glasgow, over the last ten years, a number of organisations with connections to urban agriculture have emerged, many in low-income neighbourhoods. There are a number of factors that may relate to this: Glasgow's health record is very poor, with a high rate of obesity and early mortality (the underlying socio-economic factors being described as the 'Glasgow Effect'); large tracts of land lie undeveloped in the heart of many low-income communities in outlaying areas of the city such as Toryglen, Milton and Drumchapel; access to food is frequently limited to large supermarkets that are not within walking distance for many shoppers.

....

Re-connecting

Many residents in these communities are looking for ways to re-skill themselves and re-connect with civic society after generations of unemployment and lack of opportunity. It is perhaps this feeling of crisis that has spurred communities into action, and led to the development of community projects driven by charitable and voluntary organisations. Local government, though supportive in principle, is not yet taking action. Project success is very much reliant on the enthusiasm of individuals rather than strategic or economic support.

Access to healthy food appears to be less of an urgent problem in the Netherlands. Many urban agriculture community/art projects exist, often organised by small, prosperous, middle-class groups of citizens in established neighbourhoods or 'shared streets'. Such groups are usually well-informed about the value of good nutrition, and see urban agriculture as a new kind of private leisure.

In low-income areas of The Hague, however, there is plenty of dissent and dissatisfaction, but there are fewer instances of citizen action. The restructuring of neighbourhood areas has led to high levels of 'churn', with local populations continually in flux. As such, social cohesion is poor. However, despite the challenges, a rapidly growing network of pioneering green initiatives is beginning to operate in The Hague, for example Edible Park, Foodscape Schilderswijk, the Pander Square Project and the Local Urban Nature Center.

Research over the years has shown that low-income communities are typically fragmented by shifting populations, racial tensions, lack of investment, poor planning and low expectations. For many years, artists have been seeking to raise awareness of these issues and to explore innovative solutions. Urban agriculture has been embraced by artists as a way of engaging with communities, working with them to visualise ways of improving their neighbourhoods, testing out different models and means of growing produce, and helping to create solid connections between people and places.

We have found that in both Glasgow and The Hague, local community experiences of working with artists are generally positive. Projects established in low-income communities are often highly innovative in their outlook, have a strong creative element to their programmes and are frequently led by artists or other creative practitioners on a long-term basis. For example, Love Milton, Urban Roots, Foodscape Schilderswijk (see page 81) and the Pander Square Project were led by artists, while in Glasgow, The Hidden Gardens and Sow and Grow Everywhere, a new organisation set up to support and develop urban agriculture projects, was started initially by arts organisation NVA.

We spoke with many project members who felt that artists, and art projects, play a very important role in visualising 'what is possible'. Art projects, it is felt, can 'get away with' things that other initiatives would not be able to.

....

Project Longevity

Once community art-based projects have tested the boundaries, have broadened horizons and engaged communities, what should happen next? How can such projects be scaled up, evolve, and become mainstream and sustainable in the long term?

Artists often play a role in creating bridges between groups of people and interests, which is one possible reason why artists and arts organisations have played a key role in the creation and development of urban agriculture initiatives. However, they have not demonstrated much impact on strategy or policymaking. Politicians, planners, economists and farmers must all work in partnership to embed these ideas into the infrastructure of a city.

Is it the case, as has been suggested, that artists are often brought in to make quick fixes and gloss over more complex challenges? This has reportedly happened on numerous occasions, usually involving spaces that await development as building projects stall and developers, awaiting more profitable times, 'land bank' their undeveloped sites. These sites in limbo can become unsightly dumping grounds and, rather cynically it may seem, local government interest in creating temporary urban agriculture projects in such spaces can certainly be seen as a quick fix solution.

In Glasgow, for example, there has been funding for temporary changes to 'stalled spaces'. The Dutch government has recently been offering substantial funds to 'Krachtwijken' (so-called Power Neighbourhoods) and creative projects that aim to tackle social problems rooted in urban and environmental planning. While these initiatives may give artists and communities opportunities to make a positive impact on these spaces in the short term, they don't usually fix the problem. Worse, such short-term stop gaps can lead to unrealistic expectations from all sides as to what artists can be expected to achieve.

It takes time to develop and build trust with communities, and urban agriculture projects – which literally take time to grow – rarely offer instant engagement opportunities. Urban agriculture projects initiated by or in collaboration with artists have been shown to be more meaningful and constructive if a fixed group of people takes on project organisation in the long term, working with committed partners and funding streams. What is needed is a framework for partnership working that embeds local government and urban planning stakeholders in a vision to substantially improve the access of urban communities to affordable, healthy food.

Reflecting on the future for artists working in urban agriculture, it seems likely that artists will remain a feature of many projects, especially those in low-income communities, as long as there are opportunities to connect people through food. Artists should also be part of a strategic discussion on feeding our cities in partnership with environmental organisations, policy developers, planners and politicians. Artists will always seek to maintain a level of independence, and continue to visualise creative, alternative and innovative ways of integrating urban agriculture into the urban fabric and community life.

Our research is on-going and exploratory, raising as many questions as it does answers. Like the practice of urban agriculture itself, we do not strive for one conclusion or solution, but continually test ideas, challenging our perceptions about the world we live in.

....

Alex Wilde is a visual artist based in Glasgow

....

Annechien Meier is an installation artist based in The Hague

....

www.alexwilde.info
www.annechienmeier.nl
www.agrowingexchange.com
www.lovemilton.org
www.urbanroots.org.uk
www.thehiddengardens.org.uk
www.urbaniahoeve.nl
www.sowandgroweverywhere.org
www.nva.org.uk

The Trauma of Zagreb's Torn Trees

A much loved – and recently lost – community garden in Zagreb will hopefully be re-created on its original site. This garden's story highlights the powerful need felt within many communities for a place to express their shared everyday pleasures and practices.

....

Sonja Leboš

Zagreb, capital of Croatia, assumed its present form at the end of the 19th century. The Zagreb School of Architecture, a strong modernist movement whose members were pupils of Otto Wagner, friends with Adolf Loos and co-workers of Le Corbusier, further developed the city in the 1930s. Thanks to the progressive city planners of the period and a number of international urban development competitions, a vision of New Zagreb continued to grow, interrupted only by the tragedy of World War II.

(New) Zagreb crossed the river Sava, once a barrier to further development, and spawned numerous settlements housing a great many people: Siget, Zaprude, Utrine, Travno ... to mention just the oldest. Travno, for example, a neighbourhood with 1,400 apartments built in the early 1970s, is home to one of the largest buildings in the former state of Yugoslavia. The citizens nicknamed this edifice *Mamutica* (from the word 'mamut', meaning mammoth). In front of the building, the largest in south-east Europe, the original plans proposed a great park; a vision still unrealised.

Parkless, the 1970s residents took matters into their own hands and began to plant trees and create small gardens in the open spaces in front of *Mamutica*. The oldest walnut tree on this site was planted more than 30 years ago. What started as a leisure activity became a popular neighbourhood project, with patches of land gradually turned into orchards and gardens, fenced by *Forsythia* bushes. All the construction in these gardens, even the improvised greenhouse, made use of recycled items. To the residents, these gardens were alternative homes, popular for long afternoons and weekends of socialising and growing.

....

A Way of Life
The gardens had a therapeutic impact in many ways. When in the late 1990s pension cuts bit deep across Croatia, many people were forced to live on the edge. Groceries in the supermarkets were (and still are) more expensive than in nearby Austria, where average incomes are much higher. The opportunity to grow fresh vegetables became much more than a hobby for many *Mamutica* residents; food cultivation literally became a way of life.

In February 2012, a group of young people from the area started to hang around their elderly neighbours, trying to learn more about urban gardening in order to understand a new movement – the ecological design system known as permaculture – that really interested them. But in March 2012, city officials announced their decision to finally implement the original plan for the neighbourhood's development. The growing site would be cleared in a two-week period, and the long-forgotten park created soon after.

The residents were not consulted on what kind of spaces they needed and wanted, nor were they included in discussions about the park's form or character. No-one heard about any public competition for the park design, a common practice in Zagreb, and the lack of a public framework for advancing the project worried the residents. The present mayor of Zagreb, Milan Bandić, asserted his authoritarian will, and in one afternoon the gardens which had been nurtured for decades simply vanished, the demolition tearfully observed by the long-time gardeners. Some vowed to plant their gardens again on another empty lot in the neighbourhood. Many others said they felt too weary to begin again, and simply gave up.

Picture 1/2/3/4 Vanishing gardens in Zagreb

All that remains is the slight hope that the elderly gardeners were able to pass on their knowledge to the young enthusiasts who came to seek advice at the last moment. Tonka Maleković, a visual artist who memorialised the garden's last afternoon in a series of photos, rightly pointed out that any contemporary design for the site should have incorporated the existing orchards, gardens, fruit trees and neatly planted spring onion-beds.

Urban activist and writer Saša Šimpraga suggests that, in the case of a huge building like *Mamutica*, any nearby park needs to serve all members of the community. The future park is part of the so-called Blue Horseshoe, a stretch of planned public parks designed for New Zagreb in the tradition of the central Green Horseshoe, one of the oldest planned parks in the city. Šimpraga supports the public view that the design of the new park should be opened up to all in the form of a new public competition, and that a parallel initiative for a new community garden in the neighbourhood is an obvious necessity.

....

New Initiatives
A new community garden could spread southwards of the planned park, providing growing patches for local kindergartens and schools, supported by space for holding courses on organic gardening for local residents.

To date, there have been several initiatives supporting urban agriculture in Zagreb, and recently they joined forces and issued a petition – signed by a thousand citizens so far – requesting a site for a new, albeit temporary community garden, open to all citizens and managed by locals. This alliance has proved to be a powerful force and continues to initiate campaigning activities as well as offering *pro bono* support to the citizens wishing to learn more about permaculture.

The question of how to engage with, and ultimately empower, local citizens in the design and planning of cities remains a key – and unresolved – issue in sustainable development. Design concepts must provide space for the inclusion and expression of common community practices, which always spark and grow much more quickly than the lumbering bureaucracy that exists to regulate civic behaviours. Successful city administrations must aim to identify, understand and enable the entrepreneurial practices that drive equitable growth and provide a foundation for community cohesion.

....

Sonja Leboš is an urban anthropologist, and founder of the Association for Interdisciplinary and Intercultural Research (AIIR) in Zagreb in 2002

....

www.uiii.org

Tokyo, a fruitful city
Tokyo Local Fruit is exploring how, where and by whom fruit and vegetables are being grown and eaten across the sprawling city of Tokyo. By following everyday tastes, stories and memories, this project uncovers a wealth of innovative social activity.

....

Chris Berthelsen, Jared Braiterman and Jess Mantell

Picture 1 & 2 Fruit trees growing freely across the city

Despite its image as an asphalt jungle, Tokyo continues to produce a wide variety of fruits and vegetables, as it has for hundreds of years. Trace the history of the city, and you will find that its concept of urban beauty includes all things natural.[1] In Edo times (1603-1868), Tokyo was a city of one million people living in an environment even denser than today's.[2] Samurai turned their sizeable residences into cash-producing small farms. Wrapped in living green and flowers, the doorways and back yards of Edo homes were lined with potted bonsai. In summer, morning glory and flowering gourd vines climbed the facades, nurturing a rich, imaginative nature.[3] Today, there are mature persimmon, plum, fig, and loquat trees growing freely across the city (Pictures 1 & 2).

Is Tokyo fruit a relic of the past? What is its relevance to the present? Tokyo's continual process of urban renewal demolishes old buildings and turns gardens into parking lots. Vending machines are critical nutrition input stations, and chain restaurants offer 'grandma's recipes' produced by major food companies.[4] Yet there is still a tremendous urban memory of food production, with seniors who are adept at growing and foraging local fruit.

Young people in Tokyo today face an environment very different from the abundance of the economic bubble years, and many seek a new type of economy and lifestyle that is more local, artisanal, and do-it-yourself. Tokyo fruit is less sustenance and more pleasure. It's a delicious means for inventive and social activities rooted in a deep relationship with the soil.[5] Such energy can still be found in every neighbourhood, extending outwards from Showa-era backyards, Shinto shrines, riverbanks, and across all kinds of public spaces.

Picture 3 Watermelon balcony
Picture 4 Grape covered house in central Tokyo
Picture 5 Blackberry covered house in Nakano
Picture 6 Informal raspberry construction in Nakano

....

City Fruit Paths (Figure 1)

In early 2012, we began Tokyo Local Fruit with an online survey, personal story collecting, and research studies of digital and traditional media. The project uncovers and articulates the existing and potential 'fruit paths' of the mega city, illustrating a diverse mix of land use, fruit species, food preparation and consumption practices, and sharing networks rich in stories, relationships, skills, and knowledge.

Initial results revealed over 35 types of fruit growing across Tokyo, on balconies, in gardens and houses, on rented plots, in streets, in pocket parks and in public spaces (Pictures 3, 4, 5 & 6). Plots are both intentional and accidental, offering self-grown or foraged specimens including the familiar citrus, peaches, pears, yuzu (an aromatic Japanese citrus), blueberries, plums and chestnuts; along with many surprising and mysterious species (feijoas, Japanese bayberry, mountain cherries). Persimmons are the symbol of Tokyo's fruit life (20 of the 32 responses to our preliminary survey mention the fruit[6]), and can be seen peeking over fences through autumn and winter. Says architect Tsukamoto Yoshiharu of Atelier Bow-Wow: 'When you squeeze this city, juice is sure to come pouring out...'.[7] He is speaking of Tokyo's urban space, but this is also true in a literal sense. The persistence of nature reveals Tokyo as liveable and human-scaled, hands-on and succulent: a surprising fruit basket of taste and interaction.

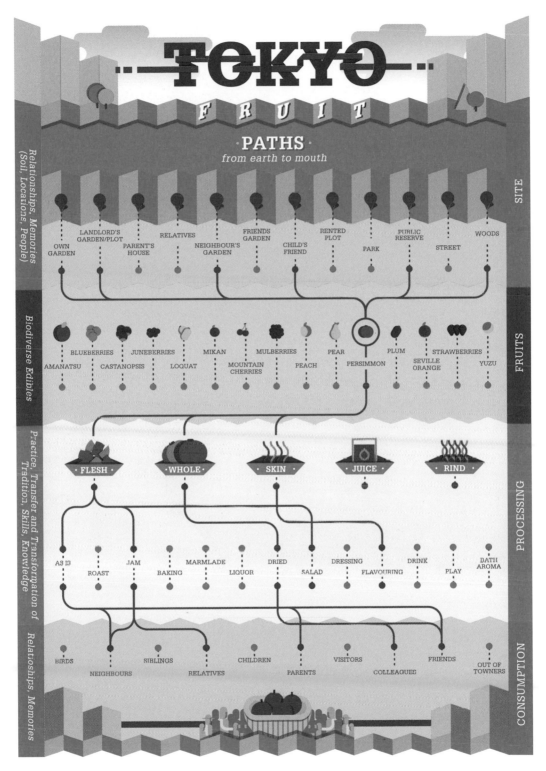

Figure 1 Tokyo Fruit Paths (with Persimmon Focus)

Picture 7
Neighbourhood Conflict: Elementary schoolchildren eating themselves sick on sour citrus soon become the focus of intra-block stress, with irate mothers hassling the fruit tree owner for compensation. Overhanging branches and fallen, rotting fruit can create slow burning grudges over sunlight and maintenance. Greedy fruit bludgers sneak away with more than their share while the home owner is away at work. These examples show that even non-edible parts of the tree contribute to the collective city's experience. This aspect of community life emerges as a common but negotiated human experiment – engaged with and 'felt' rather than delegated to local authorities or the police.

Picture 8
Inter-species Relationships: Across Tokyo, simple fruit and wire constructions invite bird life down to the human level, adding song and offering a glimpse of the intense pleasure that birds take in consuming sweet citrus. The case of an elderly man, charged by local police for using citrus to lure protected birds into his garden cages as pets, illustrates the role that fruit can play in an ageing, increasingly lonely society.

Picture 9
Play: Sturdy mulberry trees all over Tokyo ripen in late June to encourage joyous, dirty-face-and-hand climbing, chewing, spitting, throwing and feasting. Picking fruit from the tree in a casual, non-commercial setting (as opposed to a 10,000 yen, out-of-town day trip) encourages experimentation, taste-testing at different stages of ripening, and intense, adventurous non-directed play.

Picture 10
Training Fruit Thieves: Stories abound of elderly Tokyo citizens attempting to teach the younger generations the ways of the 'kaki dorobou' (persimmon thief). Convenience, regulation and scare tactics deprived a whole generation of the joys of 'free fruit now'. New attempts to show that spontaneous pleasure need not be restricted to permission-based transactions are very welcome...

Picture 11
Business and Pleasure. A bountiful persimmon tree in a busy
central Tokyo publisher's home/office space facilitates fruitful
distribution to Tokyo's 23 wards and beyond. Waste is
eliminated. Workers and visitors bring stories from the day
back home with the sweet souvenir. A treasured annual ritual
sets in, tracing consumption, work and personal relationships.

Picture 12
Reintroduction: As part of the Tokyo Local Fruit experiment, we
harvested hassaku oranges from the garden of a closed-down
school (increasingly common in Japan's ageing society) and
organised a marmalade-making event. Dormant fruit was
introduced back into the neighbourhood fruit paths, and the
finished product ended up as far as 50km away on the western
outskirts of the city.

When tracing fruit paths, from source through to processing, consumption and sharing,
it is easy to appreciate the interconnection and diversity of the soil, humans, animals, and
fruit. Tracing these paths sparks the imagination and adds a sense of living history to
routine neighbourhood walks. Is that a citrus you see peeking over the fence? Is it a
sugary sweet, or an aromatic for a relaxing bath? Or maybe it is a source of inter-mom
conflict and slow-burning grudges, (Picture 7)[9], or even the lure in a bird-catching plot?
(Picture 8).

....

Commitment to Community
Experiencing the city every day through fruit paths helps us to re-imagine what urban life
was, is, and can be. Fruit trees are not immediately productive, they have a role in the
biodiversity of the city that is historical, social and long-term. Planting a fruit tree today
signals a commitment to the community and the soil. For example, a persimmon tree may
take eight years to begin producing fruit, but once mature, a tree creates more fruit than
a single household can consume, encouraging sharing and a quest for new ways of

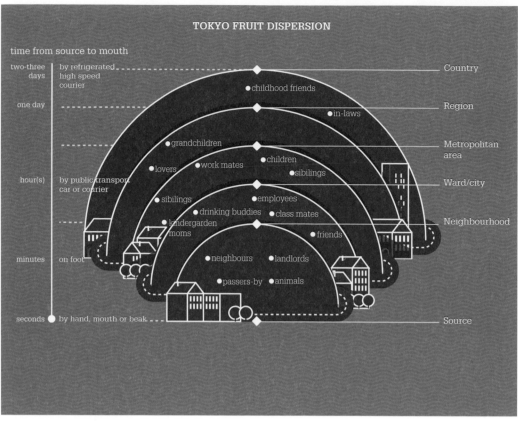

Figure 2 Tokyo fruit travels well

enjoying the fruit. Tokyo persimmons are jammed, dried, eaten as-is, added to salads, or used as a flavouring for infused spirits. Other inventive uses for Tokyo fruit include yuzu-bathing, fruit wine, tsukemono (pickles) and play (Picture 9). Acquiring the skills to grow, forage, or steal (see Picture 10), then pickle, jam, and make liquor or bath aromatics is both a source of pride and an opportunity for commerce (the exchange of savoir-faire and savoir-vivre), friendship and knowledge transformation in a (s)low-key 'homebrew revolution'.[8]

....

Tokyo Fruit Dispersion

Social consumption need not be collocated. Supported by bicycle-friendly neighbourhoods, efficient public transport, and fast and reliable food-dedicated courier services[10], Tokyo fruit travels well and fast (Figure 2) and is enjoyed by neighbours, siblings, relatives, parents, visitors, colleagues (Picture 11), and out-of-town friends. Taste tests, shopping bags, and prepared treats disperse fruit within neighbourhoods (Picture 12) and across the metropolis, radiating out to the suburbs. Cardboard boxes laden with kilogrammes of whole fruit make their way to the countryside. Knowing that local fruit is on the move, all around you, adds depth and tenderness to a city of stacked highways, concreted rivers, nondescript bedroom suburbs and ankle-deadening commuter routes.

Knowing how fruits are used gives us a glimpse into the culture that nurtures them. Tokyo's informal urban agriculture transcends functionality, utility and technique. Its landscape is humane. This city has vast potential for being a centre of fruit production, and understanding its fruit makes the life of the city more social and resilient. Eating and sharing local fruit connects us with hundreds of years of urban history. Planting fruit trees today is a promise that our future food will be shared and will always be available in the places that we walk and live in.

....

Chris Berthelsen is a researcher, designer, maker, publisher, and consultant

....

Jared Braiterman is a design anthropologist studying nature in Tokyo

....

Jess Mantell is a multidisciplinary designer exploring ways of creating more sustainable, functional, and enjoyable urban experiences

....

www.a-small-lab.com
www.tokyogreenspace.com
www.jessmantell.com

Getting started: how to pilot a successful food project

It's never easy to attract attention, secure funding or get local politicians on your side. Floor de Sera-de Jong and Simone Plantinga outline some simple strategies that will help to get your community project off the ground.

....

Floor de Sera-de Jong and Simone Plantinga

Imagine this … you feel really concerned about all the negative news across the media about children's health. Obesity rates are going up rapidly, as is the number of children suffering from diabetes. You know that this is probably related to poor eating habits, both at home and at school. The media keep suggesting that children raised in families living in socially deprived neighbourhoods frequently don't have easy access to healthy food.

This alarming situation is due to a lack of clear information about diet and health; to poor education and to the challenge of 'making do' on low incomes. The result is a lack of social equity; a society in which the calories available per head are nearly twice those needed to sustain a healthy life, and where half the food we produce is wasted, suggests Carolyn Steel, author of *Hungry City* (see page 16). And the practical outcomes? A society in which one third of the population is obese, one seventh lives on food stamps, and in which one in five restaurant meals is bought from a car, according to the report *Meal Time in Less Time* by the University of Idaho, USA.

Simple common sense suggests that the production of cheap, often pre-packed, food is neither environmentally friendly nor economically sustainable for a global urban population. So as a responsible and socially engaged civilian, and perhaps a parent too, you start thinking: but what can I actually *do* to change this for the better?

The good news is that it is possible to make a difference. Networks of concerned parents across the world are talking to their children's teachers; and discovering that school staff are also worried. They are getting together and organising brainstorms, and coming up with brilliant ideas: for example, why not create a school kitchen that can provide healthy produce for the children's meals? The garden would be near the school, and the children could help to grow the vegetables themselves. They could learn about re-using waste in the garden, or turning it into bio-energy. It's a great initiative; and you want to get going straight away.

At first, the project seems relatively straightforward. What could be difficult? The parent-teacher networking team has great skills to call upon, including excellent communicators who have no problems putting their ideas onto paper. Through the network, it is possible to generate plenty of enthusiasm and motivated helpers to work on sourcing the necessary ingredients: a space for the kitchen and garden, kitchen equipment, seeds to begin growing the crops, and a cookbook on how to cook together with children. Surely only a small amount of money is needed to get such a project off the ground? Since this project can be described as a public project, it seems natural to turn to your local authority for funding. The group prepares a detailed letter, asking for support, and including a well-written project plan. The letter is sent – and the waiting begins.

It is at this stage that the reality of local government administrative processes becomes apparent. After waiting for a while, the team leader picks up the phone and dials the number of the Department of Education, in order to find out what has happened to the proposal. The civil servant who answers the phone is friendly: 'I like your idea, but we only fund projects in terms of educational results. A school kitchen and garden clearly are not educational.' He gives your team some contacts for his colleagues at other local government departments: health care, environment, social services or economic innovation.

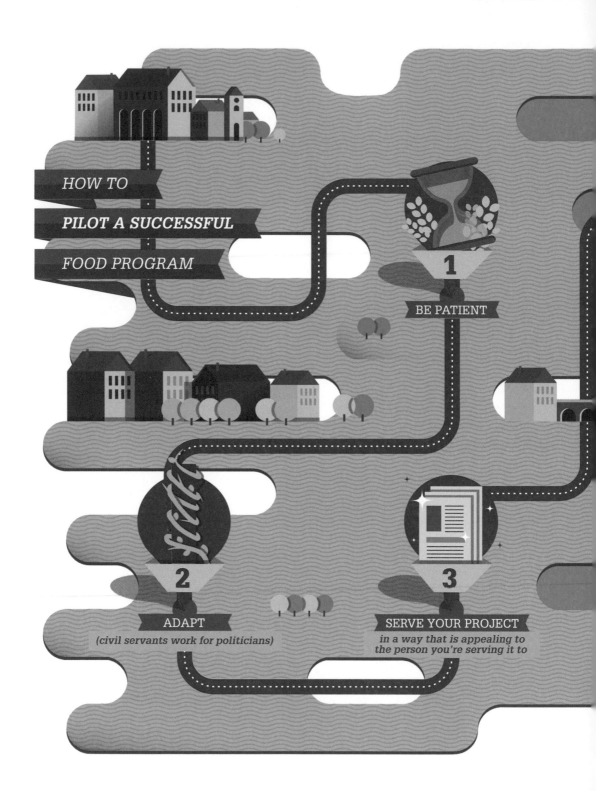

Figure 1 How to pilot a successful food program

Local government officers frequently suggest that teams seeking funding contact the national government. But with luck, initial responses at the local level will be met with enthusiasm. The local representative may phone his colleagues for you, or he may send the necessary emails to his colleagues himself. Either way, the project suddenly seems a little more complicated. At this stage, many applicants begin to wonder how they can find their way around the system.

Projects become complicated by the ways in which governmental and political systems are organised. The problem is not that the governments do not like these kind of projects, and their benefits. In fact, most national governments and many local governments are very much in favour of social entrepreneurs, especially when they address societal challenges such as the problem of unhealthy youth lifestyles.

But different levels of government, as well as different departments, frequently operate in discrete silos with little cross-departmental working, a principle intended to make the government more effective and efficient. Departments, budgets and personnel are divided according to tasks and outputs. In the Netherlands the bottom line is accountability: a particular team is responsible for specific deliverables. To many civil servants, this means only taking on projects that have been assigned to them.

So what is the best approach when dealing with local, regional or national government? First of all, be patient. Governments are slow to adjust to new ideas; to respond to emerging societal needs. Not because employees are unprofessional, but because they operate according to political systems controlled by democratic means. These systems are highly risk-averse, and much is at stake when mistakes are made. So avoid impatience or annoyance, and simply explain the project, and answer any questions that may arise, again and again as calmly as possible.

Secondly, try to adapt the project goals to match those of the local authority officer handling the matter. To find out about bigger political sensibilities, investigate the particular ambitions of the local politicians that the officers serve. Try to find out what ministers or aldermen have recently said about subjects relating to the specific area of interest. Maybe he or she is concerned about social inclusion, or wants to develop more green space within the city. Maybe the city aims to reduce CO_2, or to get more involved in local-for-local economy initiatives.

Thirdly, try framing the issues in new ways: Wayne Roberts, initiator of the Toronto Food Policy Council, uses the metaphor of a 'dessert tray' to illustrate this approach. Serve up the project in a way that is appealing to the person concerned. Luckily, food-related projects touch upon many contemporary issues and can be presented in a range of creative ways. So, if chocolate pudding is not appreciated, serve up the project as an apple pie, or perhaps ice cream and fresh fruit. Offer a range of options to choose from so individuals can decide to engage or not, based on their preferences; present the project as an educational initiative, or one to improve health or to stimulate the local economy. Either way, choose the frame depending on local context and local personalities.

Fourthly, try to find out who is actually in charge of making decisions. Most probably, the decision maker will be a politician. Try to get his or her attention. Give something in return. Will there be a grand opening for the project? If so, invite your area's local politician or decision maker to give a speech. Media moments are frequently mutually beneficial. A new field of policy is always harder to sell to public and politicians alike, so make the most of any tangible assets you have to show off, and create opportunities for politicians to make appearances.

In the fifth place, try to be smart about the results aimed for. Connect measurable benefits to the project, and view these benefits as marketable products. For example: how many children will have a better meal as a result of your initiative? How many healthy carrots will be eaten, how many families will be involved with the programme, how many farmers will be taking part? Connect these benefits to positive – and deliverable – societal goals such as healthier children, better incomes for farmers, or the increase of social cohesion in a neighbourhood.

Point six: remain alert and pay attention to detail when any support or funding arrangement is agreed. Aim to get commitment from the politician or civil servant; ideally, this will be in writing. Believe in your vision: this project is about getting people back in touch with food in a healthy, sustainable, social and economically viable manner. Food is the integrating and connecting concept in this case, a concept that can be presented in many ways in order to achieve your goals. It is a start: you are a pioneer.

Last but not least: don't give up. Yes, governments are sometimes slow, and ways of working can be difficult to grasp. There is always an election coming up, and it can be difficult to keep local officials focused on specific neighbourhood issues. Stay calm, flexible and determined! Eventually, this pilot project will set an example for others. The main cost for your team is its energy, but it is well worth the time and effort required. Good luck.

....

Floor de Sera-de Jong used to be a policy advisor on issues relating to sustainable food, European agricultural policy and regional population decline

....

Simone Plantinga is an independent advisor on food and sustainability

....

www.simoneplantinga.nl

The Selection

Introducing The Selection

Farming The City has presented a range of ideas and concepts linking sustainable urban development and the localisation of food cycles. These inspiring insights frame and underpin the book's aim: to be a demonstration of how food can play a positive role in the development of urban economics and the social and political fabric of cities.

In order to connect theory and concept to action and practice, and to underline that we need to all share freely if we are to improve the way communities function and individuals lead their lives, we have put together a showcase of inspiring and innovative projects. These are all 'works in progress' that we came across while involved with Farming the City, and each illustrates one or more ways in which food initiatives can impact positively on urban development.

For these projects, producing food is not (only) an end in itself, but also a mechanism that connects people and businesses, that creates jobs, awareness, and a sense of place, and that contributes to improved public health and a more resilient environment. This collection is a celebration of the people, organisations, businesses and policymakers that are scouting out the transition to resilient living. We have deliberately focused on projects from the global north so that the political, economic and cultural contexts remain somewhat comparable with the emerging political and economic conditions outlined in the first section of the book.

Each project has been placed within an urban development framework and 'tagged' with one or more of seven infographic labels to indicate its key dynamics:

 Social: the project creates or strengthens communities and social ties, and/or supports communication and cohesion.

 Economic: the project creates jobs, supports local economic activity and/or promotes a viable business model.

 Education: the project teaches food skills and promotes awareness about food, health, and the environment.

 Environmental: the activities are sustainable or beneficial to the environment in terms of nature, waste, energy, soil, water and air.

 Health: the project provides affordable, nutritious, fresh and healthy food and supports a positive public health agenda.

 Infrastructure: the project contributes to the food infrastructure in terms of growing sites, transportation, community platforms and/or planning.

 Liveability: the project creates interactive spaces, helps to reduce anti-social behaviour and provides urban amenities from cultural events and cafés to attractive and edible green space.

AgroCultures Nomadic /
Nomadi AgroCulture
Rome, Italy

. . . .

Starting date
October 2010

Status
In progress

. . . .

. . . .

The AgroCulture Nomadic project organises the collective harvesting of publicly available edible fruits and vegetables (for example olives, oranges, capers, rucola, chicory) growing wild in Rome's gardens and parks, public spaces and urban corners that have survived sprawl and speculation.

To date, there have been three olive harvests in different city locations organised by interested citizens: the first public harvest produced more than 300 kg of olives, which in turn made 32 litres of good oil; Olio PU.RO. In January 2011, bitter oranges were harvested for marmalade production – an activity also intended to denounce the exploitation of African workers in the farming of south Italy (Rosarno), one year earlier.

Googlemaps is used to post and share project information and to organise the harvesting groups.

The project's main driver is a kind of 'landscape activism', aiming to improve social cohesion through sharing public spaces, thinking about how urban space is used, and encouraging citizens to take responsibility for public produce. It reclaims urban space through the practice of farming, and reconnects the urban and agricultural dimensions, reminding us that cities can be rich sources of fresh food. The project is promoted by Stalker-PrimaveraRomana.

. . . .

www.pimaveraromana.wordpress.com

Agrowculture.org
New York, USA

. . . .

Starting date
October 2012

Status
Start-up

. . . .

. . . .

Agrowculture.org is a food-tech start-up that aims to change the way people grow, buy and sell their food. Urban farmers use an online marketplace to sell food directly to their neighbours, and also produce and market small-scale growing technologies. To jump-start the neighbourhood food movement, agrowculture.org is mapping urban farms and collecting 'urban farm petitions' from communities all over New York City. By tracking the demand for local food, they help growers understand their community and establish a connection with their buyers: They say: 'Our efforts are grassroots, our intentions noble and our hunger insatiable.'

The term 'local' is becoming harder to define, but it is hard to deny that food grown around the block is anything but local. Yet agrowculture.org prefers the term 'hyper-local'. With thousands of eligible rooftops, vacant lots, parking structures, vertical surfaces and stalled construction sites in cities across the world, urban agriculture has the potential to transform the way we interact with food. By closing the gap between the point of production and the point of consumption, the lifecycle of our food is shortened; obviously eliminating packaging and reducing the energy used for transport and storage. Hobbyists, gardeners, beekeepers, mycologists and brewers already share the fruits of their labours with their families and friends. If this informal exchange of goods were approached through a more systematic framework, a hyper-local food economy could emerge: decentralised production and distribution networks supporting community cohesion and dietary improvements.

. . . .

www.agrowculture.org

Almere Oosterwold
Almere, Zeewolde, The Netherlands

. . . .

Starting date
February 2011,
is addressed in the
Concept Structure
Vision Almere 2.0
in 2009

Status
The development strategy
complete, implementation
will start 2013

. . . .

. . . .

Almere Oosterwold is in the process of becoming
a unique green living and working environment.
Nearly 50 per cent of the area will be given over to
urban farming. The development strategy consists
of a simple framework together with a set of design
codes that can enable most kinds of development.
For the first time, on such a large scale, the
individuals getting involved will determine for
themselves how their houses, businesses, and even
the landscape will be created across the entire area.
This includes not only the residential buildings and
businesses, but the entire framework; local
infrastructure, water storage, sanitation, energy
supply, urban farming and public spaces

Because private initiatives will determine progress
and the rate of building, outcomes are uncertain.
The Oosterwold strategy is far from a traditional
plan; it represents the introduction of an important
new kind of development process.

. . . .

www.almere20.almere.nl/gebiedsontwikkeling/
almere_oosterwold

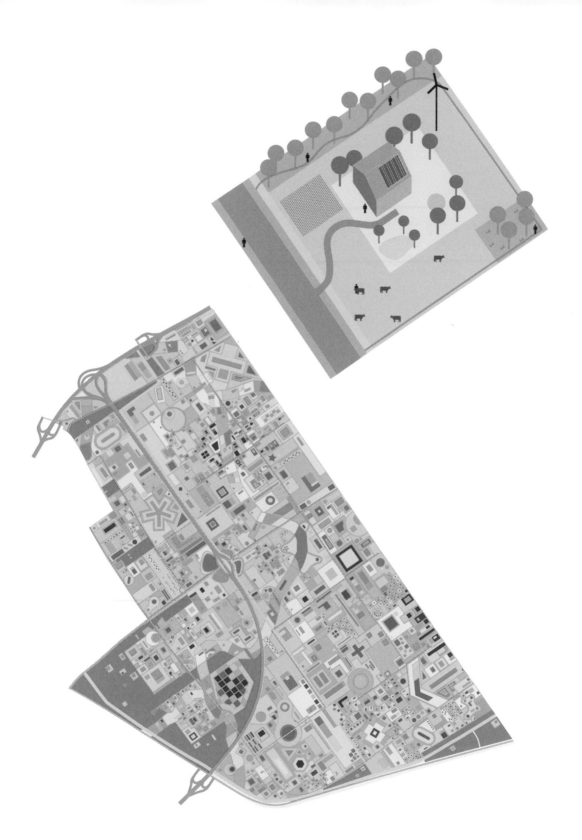

B-line Urban Delivery
Portland, USA

. . . .

Starting date
October, 2012

Status
In progress

. . . .

. . . .

B-line Urban Delivery redefines inner city freight logistics. It uses electric-assisted tricycle trucks to deliver products ranging from produce and fresh bread to office supplies and bicycle parts throughout the urban core of Portland, Oregon, USA. They specialise in fulfilling last-mile deliveries into the city, and on the way back to the hub they take fresh and healthy produce and hard to recycle items out of the city. To date, they have displaced over 20,000 truck or van-based deliveries, and helped their community avoid the mounting congestion, pollution, and costs of traditional vehicles. They are on their way to creating a more liveable community.

It is B-line's belief that the urbanisation being experienced across the globe presents the world both with incredible opportunities and significant challenges. As urban centres become more populated and developed, the demands on transportation systems and infrastructure will only increase. B-line's model, using a fleet of electric-assisted tricycles to move goods and services throughout an inner core, is a solution serving a growing demand in the marketplace without detrimentally impacting the congestion, carbon footprint or liveability of urban centres.

B-line's business model also fulfils social needs: it creates jobs and encourages fiscal responsibility and financial growth. People want to live, work, and thrive in communities that are intent on sharing access to the elements that make them unique and exciting. After three years of operating in the streets of Portland, B-line has challenged the paradigms that transportation systems are built around. Without companies and communities looking forward to what 'could be', local development issues will become mired in social inequity, environmental degradation, and disconnection. A vibrant community should be connected and sustainable, and B-line is happy to do its part.

. . . .

www.b-linepdx.com

Bee Urban
Throughout Stockholm, Sweden

....

Starting date
February 2012

Status
In progress

....

....

Bee Urban, founded by environmentally conscious biologists Karolina Lisslö & Josefina Oddsberg, arranges for the sponsorship, placement and upkeep of urban beehives. Its aim is, besides pollinating the city, to spread awareness about the impact of bees and pollination on a local and global scale.

Bee Urban's hives are placed primarily on rooftops around the city, either on sponsors' property or in locations organised by Bee Urban. The honey is packaged to reflect the sponsors' initiative for supporting environmental innovation in a positive and tangible manner, and sold, with profits re-invested in the project.

Bee Urban is reconnecting urbanites with nature in order to raise awareness about the frequently unsustainable management of the ecosystem services that we depend upon. Bee activity is crucial for the maintenance of thriving urban greenery and for balanced ecosystems that support urban food cultivation. For example, recent reports from ecologists have suggested that several plant species in the National Urban Park of Stockholm were threatened with extinction because of lack of pollinators.

....

www.beeurban.se

Brook Park Chickens
New York, USA

....

Starting date
September 2011

Status
Finished coop;
ongoing chicken run

....

....

Brook Park Chickens is a volunteer run chicken coop in New York's South Bronx, providing access to food, education and food justice. The coop of fifteen hens is managed by volunteers who share the collected eggs each week. Brook Park chickens provides a venue for children and adults to visit and learn about urban chicken keeping, where they can feed and handle the hens, and participate in the community garden.

This coop is in the South Bronx, the poorest congressional district in the United States. Almost half of all children in the area live below the poverty line. Poverty directly affects what people can buy, and what they eat. Brook Park Chickens wants its neighbours to know that, even if they are poor, they can grow their own food, raise their own chickens, and feed themselves. It wants parents and children to have the option to eat healthy, natural foods as opposed to fast foods and mass-produced pre-packaged foods, and raises the awareness of the origins of our food. The more people participate in growing their own food, the better their health and lives can be.

Brook Park Chickens brings people together and shows them how to take back control of their own food systems to get healthy food. The chickens, by the way, have their own Twitter account.

....

www.brookparkchickens.blogspot.com
The hens on Twitter: @bronxchicks

Cascina Cuccagna
Milan, Italy

. . . .

Starting date
2011

Status
In progress

. . . .

. . . .

Cascina Cuccagna is one of the oldest farmsteads in Milan, Italy, dating from 1695. In the past decade, a consortium of nine city associations developed a plan to transform the dilapidated and abandoned old homestead into a new, multi-purpose, public space. The aim was to create a meeting place and an active laboratory of culture, a point of reference for the collective pursuit of social well-being and quality of life. It is hoped that Cascina Cuccagna will showcase the role of farming in modern urban life.

Cascina Cuccagna is hosting Sustainability Milan, an innovative cultural research project analysing the sustainability exemplars run across the city by Non-Governmental Organisations (NGOs), associations, foundations and institutional bodies. Despite being a work in progress, the urban farmstead hosts several events across its 66-room building and 1,500 square metre green area.

Cascina Cuccagna educates urban dwellers about the relationships between the environment and food, culture, territory, cohesion and integration. It reminds us that we have forgotten where we come from. Just as the building was left to decay, citizens have left behind their intimate connection to food, food production, and community. The project supports activities and events to rekindle these links, such as growing traditional – and often forgotten – vegetables, a bicycle repair workshop, a store selling local produce and a restaurant serving dishes made with seasonal, handmade, local ingredients.

. . . .

www.cuccagna.org

CERES
Melbourne, Australia

....

Starting date
1982

Status
In progress

....

....

CERES (Centre for Education & Research in Environmental Strategies) is a thriving 12-acre environmental education centre set on a rehabilitated landfill site in inner city Brunswick, just 7 km from Melbourne's Central Business District. This unique city farm feeds and inspires urban farmers and eaters of all ages, abilities and backgrounds. The farm encourages people to get 'hands-on' with its demonstration local food system that includes a plant nursery, organic market gardens, a commercial aquaponics system, bees, a food market, a local organic home delivery service, community gardens, a chook (chicken) group, a local in-season catering service, an organic cafe and an urban orchard produce swap – all of which offer training and volunteer opportunities for schools and the public. The CERES organic farm is complimented by sustainable energy and water demonstrations: there are solar, wind, biogas and greywater displays on site.

CERES is an education centre and also a kind of sanctuary. As many as 400,000 people, including 70,000 school children, visit each year to take courses, to volunteer or simply to visit, wanting somewhere peaceful and positive to bring young children. CERES teachers also go out to 500 Victorian schools to run sustainability and food growing programmes, building on the learning students get on site at CERES. Our team also runs several social enterprises; it employs more than 180 people from all backgrounds and is a strong player in the local economy. Through its market, cafe and home delivery service, CERES is one of Victoria's largest buyers of organic produce, and it uses its market power to support local farmers. It also grows and sells its own produce in two market gardens and a commercial aquaponics project it has built for research and training purposes.

....

www.ceres.org.au

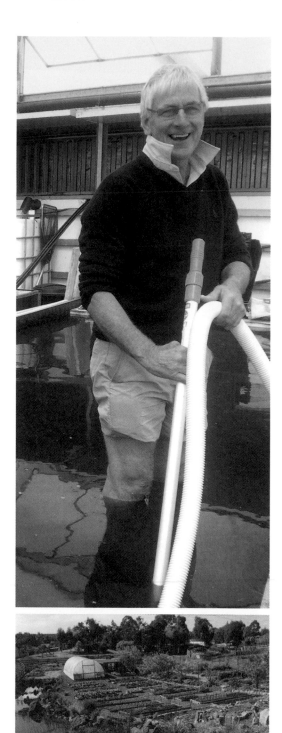

Common Good City Farm
Washington DC, USA

....

Starting date
2007

Status
In progress

....

....

Common Good City Farm's mission is to grow food, educate, and help low-income DC community members meet their food needs. It aims to serve as a replicable model of a community-based, sustainable urban food system.

Common Good City Farm's educational programmes and learning workshops provide hands-on training in food production, healthy eating and environmental sustainability. The Farm itself serves as a demonstration site for individuals, organisations and students in the DC Metro area. The site and their programmes integrate people of all ages, classes and races to create vibrant and safe communities.

Urban community agriculture can be found in cities across the country and the world. These farms and gardens not only directly provide fresh food, but also offer safe outdoor settings for learning, growing and nourishing. This relationship ultimately leads to the development of strong communities.

Common Good is located in the heart of the city. The farm is an excellent example of how we can improve the health of our environment in urban areas. Farming is done using sustainable methods composting, using rain garden full of native flowers to help control storm water run-off, and a bee hive that happily pollinates plants. Common Good serves as a source of fresh fruit and vegetables in a food desert: in this neighbourhood, the nearest grocery store is over a mile away. The farm engages young people in environmental education, getting them involved in growing food and healthy eating. With 82 per cent of the US population living in urban areas, it is important to have places like Common Good City Farm to show that urban areas can develop sustainably, improve their environment and strengthen their communities.

....

www.commongoodcityfarm.org

Culinary Misfits
Berlin, Germany

....

Starting date
March 2012

Status
Start-up

....

....

Culinary Misfits is a start-up launched by Lea Brumsack and Tanja Krakowski to focus on sustainable food culture. They aim to inspire people to reduce waste and strive to change public perception with regard to natural food. Roughly 40 per cent of all grown vegetables are wasted because they are thought to be 'imperfect'; buyers consider them deformed, too small, too big, the wrong colour, or simply odd-looking. However, these 'misfits' are perfectly usable and should never be thrown away. Culinary Misfits brings the misfits back to the market and to city tables. Their motto is: 'Eat the entire harvest!'

By cooking with 'misfits', urban dwellers can reduce the amount of money and resources required to sustain a large city. Consumers are often unaware of where their produce is cultivated, and have either forgotten or never knew what natural foods look like. Lea and Tanja work together with local farmers from Berlin and the surrounding areas to cook up these natural-looking vegetables, old varieties and wild herbs into delicious and nutritious meals.

....

www.culinarymisfits.de

€4.50

Dakboerin / Rooftop farmer
Haarlem, the Netherlands

. . . .

Starting date
January 2011

Status
In progress

. . . .

. . . .

Dakboerin advises anyone interested in edible rooftops, walls, boxes or windows. The project's main goal is to grow food in as many places as possible in the city; it also inspires people to get involved in food growing, and gives support and advice to anyone wishing to do so. Dakboerin designs urban vegetable rooftop gardens; taking on the building, the planting, and even the harvesting.

Urban rooftop farming offers many benefits: it gives pleasure, produces healthy food and creates new uses for urban spaces. Rooftop farming is also a response to food scarcity, creative water management and the challenges of sustainable food distribution in cities: shorter distances travelled mean carbon reduction and less congestion. Other benefits of rooftop farms include improved use of rainwater and the creation of habitats for insects and birds.

. . . .

www.dakboerin.nl

143

DemoTuinNoord /
Demonstration Garden
Amsterdam North, the Netherlands

....

Starting date
September 2011

Status
In progress

....

....

Urbaniahoeve's Demonstration Garden is a
showcase of Urbaniahoeve's research areas,
including growing foodscapes into the national
ecological framework, phytoremediation (cleaning
soils of contaminants with plants, soil biota, and
mycelia), urban topsoil soil (re)generation,
closed-cycle use of (organic) materials, green
surfacing, water sequestration, espalier hedging,
façades and barriers, and terra-forming with mound
gardening (Hügel-kultuur). While the core team
participates in information-rich work, the
neighbours are attracted to the DemoGarden by
its collective, organic kitchen garden and (private)
park space (with pit oven). The 1,500 m² garden is
adjacent to a large urban park, making the ambition
of a contiguous ecological framework a realistic
endeavour.

The Demonstration Garden is a living catalogue
of Urbaniahoeve's green typologies. There the team
can test, for example, the durability of its green
paving, or how quickly local soils can be remediated,
or the time it takes to make a poor soil into a fertile
one. Working with local people and existing
materials and institutions, Demonstration Garden
has quickly built a 15-person core team with a
strong sense of project ownership, that is
knowledgeable about our green typologies and
whose members bring their own expertise to the
project. Urbaniahoeve believes that we as citizens
need to be highly skilled at creating strong
communities with sufficient knowledge to
phytoremediate contaminated urban soils (and not
simply remove and replace them), and to transform
unproductive spaces into contiguous, edible
landscapes.

....

www.urbaniahoeve.nl

The Farmery
Raleigh, North Carolina, USA

. . . .

Starting date
Research began
January 2008,
prototyping began
in October 2009

Status
Start-up

. . . .

. . . .

The Farmery is an urban farm and market built
from shipping containers and standard greenhouse
components. The lower level serves as a market
selling produce and the entire structure is used for
growing. Mushrooms are grown on the inside of the
containers and the container walls are covered in
growing panels to form living walls producing herbs,
strawberries, lettuces and greens. The Farmery
raises the value of crops through an incredible retail
experience: customers are surrounded with growing
food, they can see they are purchasing the freshest
possible produce. The Farmery lowers the costs of
production by reducing inventory loss, middle men,
packaging, storage and transportation costs.

The Farmery is a completely new approach to
farming and food retailing; one that looks for
symbiosis within the entire system rather than
for the optimisation of individual components. It's
a growing and retailing system designed to provide
locally grown food in urban neighbourhoods. Local
food needs an entirely new business model that
recognises its strengths and accommodates
weaknesses.

The Farmery has recognised how difficult it is for
supermarkets to offer locally-grown produce,
primarily because of the inconsistent supply.

The Farmery solves the issue of inconsistent supply
by growing its own produce so that it will always
have a stable supply. In this way, the Farmery can
accommodate growers who may have only very
small quantities of very specialised crops to sell.

The Farmery offers a completely new way to shop
for food; one where the story of the farmers and their
food is experienced throughout the shopping
experience. The entire structure of the Farmery is
used to grow food, so customers are surrounded by
the sights, smells, and sounds of their food growing
as they are making their purchases. This helps
customers understand and appreciate the added
value of small-scale, artisanal farming.

. . . .

www.thefarmery.com

Farmscape
Throughout Los Angeles, USA

....

Starting date
October 2008

Status
Growing, in progress

....

....

Farmscape's mission is to turn Los Angeles into a farm, one plot at a time. It helps residents, restaurant owners and institutions design, build, and maintain organic vegetable gardens across the city. The aim is to improve the city's ecological footprint, the character of the urban environment, and the food supply. Farmscape also wishes to raise expectations about urban farming by demonstrating how productive urban plots are and how delicious the food can be, and by showcasing the many social and economic benefits that such projects bring to their local communities.

Farmscape offers a new way of thinking about landscaping and an alternative logistics for local food systems. It helps people convert unused or unfarmed landscapes into thriving, beautiful farmscapes, on sites of all sizes and circumstances. Farmscape creates valuable green jobs in the city, unlocks the potential of idle land assets, and builds a top quality, transparent, super-local food supply for its membership.

....

www.farmscapegardens.com

Fermes Lufa / Lufa Farms
Montréal, Canada

Starting date
April 2011

Status
In progress

Lufa Farms is a Montreal business that grows vegetables and greens year-round in a 31,000-square-foot greenhouse atop a two-storey office building. It began selling and delivering produce to local consumers in 2011. Its greenhouse structure was the world's first commercial-scale rooftop greenhouse.

Lufa's greenhouse is able to supply 2,000 Montreal families with weekly baskets of produce, grown without pesticides, fungicides or herbicides. Deliveries are available by subscription or by ordering from the company website.

Lufa employs controlled-environment agriculture, enabling the operation to yield as much produce as a conventional farm 10 times its size. Lufa's greenhouse collects rainwater and filters and re-circulates irrigation water.

What Lufa is doing in Montreal could be an integral part of any urban centre. Cities could be self-sufficient in their food production if enough rooftops were utilised (Montreal could be self-sufficient if 28 million square feet of rooftop space were used for greenhouse production; that's roughly the area of 19 shopping centres). The average consumer is far too distant from their food sources and the link between grower and consumer must be made closer: consumers should know who their farmer is, how their food is grown, and have every assurance in the traceability and safety of the food they eat.

Lufa sees the idea of urban farming as essential to cities throughout the world, both for consumer access to fresh, safe produce, to rebalance land uses, and to eliminate unsustainable agricultural practices throughout the world.

www.lufa.com/en

Forage Kitchen
San Francisco, USA

....

Starting date
Fundraising now,
target opening
date June 2013

Status
In progress

....

....

Forage Kitchen is a co-working space for food. More than a shared kitchen, it will be a home for food makers and a hub for the Bay Area food community. It's a philosophy-focused space, where local food producers can start their projects with the support of others who are going through the same experiences. They will work together to source local produce and meats from local producers, while at the same time supporting the urban food-making/growing community. This space will be a model for other spaces worldwide. Rather than escaping to the country to change the world it is time to move into cities and change them from within.

Forage Kitchen has raised $156,000 (€121,637) via the Kickstarter online community and is now working on finding a suitable space. When the project opens, if you are starting a business, it can offer space. Office, kitchen, business support, equipment rental, preparation help and dish washing, all in one place. Need to work on a computer? Need to test a recipe? Need to make a ton of product for an event? Come to Forage Kitchen. More than a kitchen, this space will be a community of makers working side by side to create something really special. There will be retail space for products, as well as relationships with local stores to help with the confusing process of retail distribution. There will be classes, and opportunities to complete big projects on professional equipment.

This space will provide a much-needed resource for the food community of San Francisco. A space to help small businesses thrive, but also one where people can get their feet wet when deciding if making food full-time is for them. A welcoming space that will bring food makers and food lovers together under one roof. These spaces are a much-needed next step for the food movement across the country; spaces that will get us out of our cramped kitchens and bring us together around food.

....

www.foragesf.com/foragekitchen

Good Food Jobs
Online

. . . .

Starting date
October 2010

Status
In progress

. . . .

. . . .

Good Food Jobs is the first online job search engine for people seeking meaningful – as in satisfying, empowering, and beneficial to others – food-related work. It was created to strengthen the food economy by encouraging growth and exploration. The co-founders of Good Food Jobs, Taylor and Dorothy, live in Greensboro, Vermont, and Brooklyn, New York, respectively. The website is active on an international level. The site, and the accompanying gastronomes blog, are used to educate people about the multitude of ways one can embark on a food-related career. Taylor and Dorothy believe that food is the perfect outlet for fulfilling employment because it has the potential to make an impact culturally, economically, and environmentally. With thousands of jobs posted, and tens of thousands of devoted followers, they are dedicated to changing the world, one hard worker at a time.

Growth and spread are two elements of urban sustainability. Creating a website to bring people together around the common goal of working in food, for the purpose of improving one's own life and the lives of others, is Good Food Jobs' attempt to grow and spread the so-called food revolution. It believes that food-related jobs are sustainable across multiple dimensions – for the individual, for the community, and for the planet – and that our health and future depend on more people creating ideas and working to implement them. Good Food Jobs helps to bring the farm to the city, and vice versa, by informing people about how they can make a difference through their work, and by making jobs in food accessible to a wide audience.

. . . .

www.goodfoodjobs.com

Helsinki Plant Tram
Helsinki, Finland

....

Starting date
September 2012

Status
Temporary
(Project now complete)

....

....

Helsinki Plant Tram was a participatory urban intervention that took place on Helsinki's local transport network. It included a mobile garden that travelled through the city, along with an imaginative urban garden inspired by the iconic wooden roller coaster at the Linnanmäki Amusement Park. Plant tram passengers were encouraged to give 'plant donations' in place of fares, and potential sites that could add to the network of growing spaces in the Finnish capital were identified. The project was designed and produced by the London-based landscape practice Wayward Plants, in partnership with local environmental organisation Dodo. It was commissioned by the British Council for the 'Everyday Discoveries' exhibition at Souvilahti, part of World Design Capital Helsinki 2012. Following the exhibition, the garden was designed to be reconfigured into a new space housing 50-plus planters.

The Helsinki Plant Tram was an imaginative proposition for Helsinki, linking the transport systems to the growing infrastructure of urban gardening. Although the tram only operated for a few days as an urban intervention, it encouraged participation with passengers sharing stories during the journey. An on-going mobile garden, circling Helsinki on the tram route, could become a positive reality; continually evolving with the network of growing spaces in Helsinki.

....

www.planttram.org

HK Farm
Hong Kong, China

. . . .

Starting date
April 2012

Status
In progress

. . . .

. . . .

HK Farm is an organisation of Hong Kong urban farmers, artists and designers. It aims to communicate the value of rooftop farming and benefits of locally produced food.

HK Farm grows local food and designs products and services relating to urban agriculture. It is currently creating a sustainable community in Ngau Tau Kok, using an old industrial building and its rooftop.

HK Farm grows seasonally and practices organic farming methods. As part of creative, community and educational work it offers school tours, collaborates with other rooftop farms, and runs planter-making workshops and exhibitions.

From a farming perspective, Hong Kong is producing less and less food every year. For example, in 1980 20 per cent of the vegetables that were consumed in Hong Kong were grown in Hong Kong. In 2012, this figure has significantly reduced to only 2.3 per cent. It has been argued by some rural farmers that the government is not supportive of local agriculture in its policymaking; and this can be seen in a current and controversial urban development plan to relocate 10,000 villagers who live on some of the most fertile land in Hong Kong, and building on top of 98 hectares of farmland in the process.

As urban farmers, HK Farm is aware of such socio-cultural and environmental issues affecting Hong Kong and its population and aims to address them in its organic urban farming practices. For example, HK Farm's soil is from the topsoil of an organic farm called Mapopo Community Farm, located in Fanling, a rural part of Hong Kong that is scheduled for urban development. HK Farm amends, fertilises and aerates its soil with waste products from the city such as food waste from local restaurants, rice husks from Hong Kong's dehusking machine and sawdust from the wood workshop under the rooftop. It also reuses discarded wooden boxes as planters for its rooftop farm. HK Farm promotes such organic practices in its creative workshops, school tours, exhibitions and with the community around its rooftop.

. . . .

www.hkfarm.org

Incredible Edible Todmorden
Todmorden, UK

....

Starting date
February 2008

Status
In progress

....

....

Incredible Edible Todmorden is a movement of passionate people working together for a world where all share responsibility for the future well-being of people and planet. By working together, using the common language of food, we can cross cultural, social and economic barriers to create a kinder, more sustainable community.

Incredible Edible aims to provide access to good local food for all, and promotes learning from field to classroom to kitchen (preschool ages through to adult education). Incredible Edible supports local businesses and, through apprentice schemes, helps to train the food producers of the future.

Much is said about investing in a better future for all, and the past couple of years have thrown up many initiatives that can bring people closer to an understanding of the importance of good food. We need a different way of thinking: to build schools for the future that have the living, edible world at their heart; to transform health buildings with edible plants and trees as an integral part of the design and workplace; to encourage public bodies to release land for food growing, and to 'plan for food' by supporting local food production through the planning system, with all local plans identifying and providing places for growing.

Incredible Edible's suggestions:

_make growing a performance indicator for 'well-being' across all public services;
_insist all new homes to have ready-to-grow spaces;
_encourage all social landlords to allocate space for growing;
_create a charter for truly local markets – support local food producers and farmers and campaign for the reallocation of subsidies;
_make sure public bodies like schools and health authorities have procuring local food as a priority; and
_invest in food skills for the future. We need incredible degrees and diplomas, cooks and technologists, farmers and fabulous food producers.

....

www.incredible-edible-todmorden.co.uk

Kääntöpöytä /
Turntable Urban Garden
Helsinki, Finland

....

Starting date	Status
March 2012	In progress

....

....

Turntable is an open, public space in Pasila's historical railway maintenance yard, featuring an urban garden, cafe and greenhouse. It was set up by Dodo, an environmental Non-Governmental Organisation (NGO) based in Helsinki.

Dodo's urban farming movement began in this same location in 2009, when gardeners took over disused wasteland to create a productive public space. In 2012, Dodo activists transformed Turntable into an urban farming test lab and learning resource. During its first year in action, Turntable has held various workshops and events, and has offered locally-grown food in the Turntable cafe. The garden has a beehive, a dry toilet, composting sites, a cob oven and solar panels for energy production.

Turntable is located in a district in Helsinki that will see extensive future redevelopment. The project aims to develop and promote sustainable urban gardening and local food production, and to provide a site for grass roots cultural action.

....

www.kaantopoyta.fi

MushroomWall
Amsterdam, the Netherlands

....

Starting date
June 2012

Status
In progress

....

....

MushroomWall aims to recycle urban waste in the form of used coffee grounds and transform it into edible fungi. The waste is inoculated with species of fungus that can easily digest it, the result being delicious oyster or shiitake mushrooms. The vertical growing system uses recycled plastic cylinders placed in multiple locations in Amsterdam's inner city: balconies, interiors and the walls of narrow alleys. The cool, protected alleys are well-suited to mushroom cultivation, as this system requires no soil and limited maintenance, and directly transforms waste at the point of production. At the same time, the project aims to make the transformation from waste to food visible by locating the whole process in public space.

Amsterdam has more than 4,000 cafes, hotels, and restaurants that generate around 20,000 kilos of coffee grounds every day. The spent coffee is normally mixed with other trash and sent to landfills. Mushrooms are such efficient biological transformers that a quarter of the mass of the used coffee can become mushrooms. The end product of the growth cycle, besides the protein-rich mushrooms, is a rich humus super-compost.

We set out to examine all of the unused urban space that could be potentially used for this specific type of urban agriculture. The vertical growing system requires very little space, no soil, and no light. Mushroom gardens can be created where no other types of gardens could exist. Ignored and underutilised alleys and urban corners will become magical, mysterious, and nutritional destinations. The plan is to partner with restaurants and cafes who can begin to transform their own waste into food that can be used in the kitchen. Cooks will be able to walk out their door to harvest fresh mushrooms on their doorsteps. MushroomWall is a simple concept: waste = food. By making this process clearly visible, accessible, and profitable, a new sustainable and cultural cycle is added to urban life.

....

www.destuurlui.nl
www.groundcondition.com

The People's Supermarket
London, UK

....

Starting date
June 2010

Status
In progress

....

....

The People's Supermarket's vision is to create a commercially sustainable, social enterprise that achieves its growth and profitability targets whilst operating within values based on community development and cohesion. Our intent is to offer an alternative food buying network, by connecting an urban community with the local farming community.

The Supermarket is a sustainable food cooperative that responds to the needs of the local community and provides healthy, local food at reasonable prices. To this end, our team believes in a series of key values, which guide the philosophy and management approach.

TPS members join the supermarket for various reasons, but all agree that the project exists to provide an alternative. As members, we want to make consumers more aware of the various simple things they can impact on their local urban environment. Our values are reflected by the following statements: 'We are ethical, sustainable and transparent in business; respectful and responsible with resources; friendly, active and inclusive.' TPS is passionate about food, but understands that food is mainly a tool used to reach out to urban consumers, urging them to reconnect with the way their food is produced, as well as with one another. TPS sources products as locally as possible, bringing food back to the heart of the city. TPS wants to show that the status quo can be challenged, and hopes to inspire and empower urban communities. TSP is For the People, By the People.

....

www.thepeoplessupermarket.org

Prinzessinnengarten
Berlin, Germany

. . . .

Starting date
July 2009

Status
In progress

. . . .

. . . .

Prinzessinnengarten began as a pilot project at Moritzplatz in Berlin's Kreuzberg district, on a site that had been a wasteland for more than 50 years (once the location of the renowned Wertheim department store). Prinzessinnengarten not only provides fresh food and flowers for the local community, it is also a social hub in a central location. Since Prinzessinnengarten is currently using the site on a temporary lease basis, the food and flowers are planted in mobile containers.

Besides offering a wide variety of vegetables, herbs and flowers to buy from its kiosk, along with space for growing, Prinzessinnengarten has a café and restaurant and frequently hosts community events. More importantly, it also educates children, neighbours and citizens about locally grown food and sustainable living.

Prinzessinnengarten is a resource centre for a new type of resilient city that can handle future challenges (in terms of climate, resources, mobility, social cohesion, education and demographic change) using solutions that are demonstrated and tested on site. Prinzessinnengarten also employs 13 people full time during the summer.

. . . .

www.prinzessinnengarten.de

R-Urban: networks and practices of resilience
Colombes, France

. . . .

Starting date
September 2012

Status
In progress

. . . .

. . . .

R-Urban is a bottom-up strategy exploring urban resilience by introducing a network of resident-run facilities connecting key fields of activity (economy, habitat, urban agriculture, culture). The project sets a precedent for the bottom-up, participative retrofitting of metropolitan suburbs, in which the relationship between the urban and the rural is reconsidered. R-Urban initiates closed ecological cycles between the urban and the rural. The strategy is centred on the active involvement of citizens in developing collaborative practices and creating networks from the local to the regional scale.

After three years of research, R-Urban started out in 2011 in Colombes, a suburban town near Paris, in partnership with the local municipality, a number of local organisations, and local residents. It tries to show what citizens can do if they organise themselves around new facilities, and change their working and living habits to collectively address the challenges of the future. This collective production of space and urban practice, managed by citizens, is what Antonio Negri calls the 'construction of the common by the multitude'. It will necessarily challenge the existing institutional, juridical and political frameworks.

. . . .

www.r-urban.net

Rijp en Groen Tolsteeg
Utrecht, the Netherlands

. . . .

Starting date
January 2012

Status
In progress

. . . .

. . . .

Stichting Stadslandbouw Utrecht (Utrecht Urban Agriculture Foundation) turns public space into places to meet and eat. It has also developed, together with partners, edible gardens around the Tolsteeg home for the elderly. During spring 2012, a soulless lawn adjacent to the restaurant was turned into a lively garden filled with half-forgotten vegetables, herbs and flowers, each evoking memories of bygone days.

Autumn 2012 will see the development of an inner garden in the home's atrium, transforming a barren, stony space into a green oasis. The gardens create a pleasant living environment for the inhabitants of Tolsteeg, supply fresh produce for meals and during workshops and garden maintenance sessions the elderly meet with volunteers from the neighbourhood.

The set-up and structure of the Tolsteeg gardens project has been key to its success; bringing together a range of stakeholders in a step-by-step approach to transformation. Agnes Looman, a herborist with roots in care for the elderly, drew plans for the outdoor garden. TU Delft's design graduate team Logee provided expert input with regard to the technical possibilities for the complex atrium and artist, gardener and cook Kees Tuint designed the inner garden and supports the garden team. Through his incredible knowledge of plants, coupled with great social skills, he has engaged inhabitants, volunteers and staff in the project.

Early commitment was earned by building on incremental insights and feedback during the creation process, staying in touch with the people involved, and avoiding over-defining the end results. The project commissioners – housing corporation Portaal, the City of Utrecht and AxionContinu, organisation for care for the elderly – were quickly infected by enthusiasm. Each was clearly able to imagine the added value that urban farming could bring to the realisation of their own aims; creating a better living environment, strengthening the connection between the home and its surroundings, improving levels of well-being and providing fresh food for the inhabitants.

. . . .

www.urbanpilots.wordpress.com

179

Roppongi Nouen Farm
Tokyo, Japan

....

Starting date
2010

Status
In progress

....

....

Roppongi Nouen Farm is an urban farm in the Roppongi district in the centre of Tokyo. Set in a showcase structure consisting of eight glass containers, visitors can view vegetables grown inside the glasshouse by local farmers, and eat the fresh produce in the experimental restaurant next door that is also part of the project and is run by people from farm families. This is a place where people can interact with agriculture.

The project aims to raise community awareness of the food system through siting food cultivation in the heart of an urban city. By using glass and an 'inorganic' iron frame, the designers used a contrasting presentation that displays how food growing and the city can co-exist.

....

www.roppongi-nouen.jp

Sky Greens
Singapore

· · · · · · · · · · · ·

Starting date
October 2012

Status
In progress

· · · · · · · · · · · ·

· · · · · · · · · · · ·

Sky Greens is a low carbon, water-driven and rotating vertical commercial urban farm for tropical vegetables. It is a modular semi-automated system of multi-layered troughs in a rotating A-frame vertical structure that enables easy installation and maintenance. The vegetables are housed in greenhouses and grown in composted soil media, are harvested every day and delivered rapidly to consumers via retail outlets. The system has the potential to produce 50 per cent of Singapore's green leafy vegetables on 50 hectares of land. Using current farming methods, around 7 per cent could be produced on around 100 hectares. By early 2013, Sky Greens will be able to supply about two tons per day.

The system is characterised by low energy usage and very low water usage. All organic waste is composted and recycled. Students in applied science are involved in an educational scheme combining theory and practice on the site. All these assets make Sky Greens a system with a high potential for food production in urban environments; the highly efficient growing method that requires minimum input and outputs high yields is an innovative concept. Sky Greens provides fresh food and education, contributes to the localisation of the food system and has a low impact on the environment.

· · · · · · · · · · · ·

www.skygreens.com

Spiel/Feld Marzahn
Berlin-Marzahn, Germany

....

Starting date
August 2011

Status
In progress

....

....

Spiel/Feld Marzahn is an urban agriculture project aiming to establish community-led food growing on a redundant, 4,000 m² site in the centre of a prefabricated housing estate in the borough of Marzahn-Hellersdorft, north-east Berlin. The project is a collaboration between landscape architecture students at the Technical University Berlin, the planning department of Marzahn-Hellersdorf, and local actors on site. Key aims are to instigate spatially effective and productive use of a brownfield site, to help build community cohesion and offer different lifestyle choices. Currently, the project consists of a 600 m² growing field, a purpose-built shed and an emerging group of local gardeners.

The Berlin borough of Marzahn-Hellersdorf has many areas of under-used open urban space that frequently become management burdens for the local council. Development pressure is low, as is the level of entrepreneurship among the local inhabitants concerning new uses for these spaces. However, the council's environmental department has recently started work on a borough-wide urban agriculture strategy that will match interested urban farmers with usable land. The Spiel/Feld project is setting a spatial precedence for a certain type of agricultural use in the area, and is establishing urban food production as a valid and desirable space use option in the borough.

The Spiel/Feld project is located in a deprived area of Berlin: unemployment is high and household earnings are low. Despite the fact that the area is home to many people, there are comparatively few opportunities for leisure activities.

Urban agriculture projects have the potential to increase social productivity and raise ecological awareness. They do more than benefitting specific sites; they also encourage constructive public discourse relating to local planning issues. With these aims in mind, Spiel/Feld is run as a participatory project with inclusive decision-making practices. The project focuses on ecological education by working closely with local schoolchildren, and by providing facilities for meetings and gardening workshops.

....

www.spielfeldmarzahn.de

Sweet Water
Milwaukee, USA

....

Starting date
February 2009

Status
In progress

....

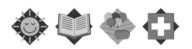

....

Sweet Water is a social business and innovation centre, advancing the commercialisation, democratisation and globalisation of aquaponics, an eco-system method of food production. Plus it offers more: it's a science lab, a school, an eco-tourist destination, an artists and tinkerers' workshop, and a community enterprise centre. Sweet Water aspires to grow urban farmers, green tech start-up businesses, beloved communities, and ... organic cities.

Sweet Water is introducing 21st-century biotechnology and information technology skillsets for learners young and old. This is a critical experiment for translating waste to resources, for example, converting empty sites and old industrial complexes to productive spaces, and unemployed and underemployed citizens to producers of basic value. These transformations provide digital and hands-on work-based learning that can help to democratise STEM training (science, technology engineering and math) across the country. Sweet Water is a hybrid enterprise experiment including Sweet Water Organics (SWO) and Sweet Water Foundation (SWF).

....

www.sweetwater-organic.com

Thijl
Amsterdam, the Netherlands

....

Starting date
April 2010

Status
In progress

....

....

Thijl is a cargo bike delivery service for organic products in Amsterdam. Using electric cargo bikes, Thijl delivers more than 1,800 products to households and businesses. The service currently delivers mainly groceries, but Thijl is looking to expand the range of organic and sustainable goods that are delivered in the near future and aims to expand the service to other Dutch cities.

Logistics – the stocking of stores and deliveries to households and businesses – imposes a great deal of infrastructural pressure on our cities. The lion's share of the typical logistics fleet produces noxious gases and is a major cause of urban congestion. Electric cargo bikes do not emit health-damaging gasses, and take up less space on the urban road system. From this perspective, it makes a lot of sense to use cargo bike delivery services where possible.

Community-scaled delivery services – flexible, quick deliveries over short distances – support small-scale food production, simultaneously boosting efficiency by enabling consumers and businesses to produce their food at home and at the office. These new logistical solutions are effectively redistributing products between urban food consumers and urban food producers throughout the city.

....

www.thijl.nl

Trädgård på Spåret /
Garden on the Track
Stockholm, Sweden

. . . .

Starting date
January 2012

Status
In progress

. . . .

. . . .

Garden on the Track is an urban community garden growing a variety of vegetables, and a space where people can learn how food grows, and how to grow food. The garden taps into the emerging food-growing culture and provides a space to grow food for people who don't have a garden of their own.

Garden on the Track is also a planting school where urbanites can learn about food and growing techniques. It has a café, a market, and space for art and events. Besides having this role as a meeting point for ecology, culture and urban development, the project aims to involve people in the on-going urban development process for the area (Vision Söderstaden 2030).

With an open membership-based community of around 400 people, the site is covered with hundreds of growing boxes.

. . . .

www.pasparet.org

UIT JE EIGEN STAD /
From Your Own City
Rotterdam, the Netherlands

....

Starting date
October 2012

Status
In progress

....

....

From Your Own City is a commercial urban food growing and preparation concept that aims at a complete vertical integration of the food chain. Everything grown at From Your Own City can be bought at its shop, and the produce is also used in its restaurant, along with regional produce. The menu changes daily, depending on the ingredients coming from the garden. Fruit, vegetables and herbs are grown, chickens scratch freely around on site, and tilapia and other fish breed in an aquaponics system.

From Your Own City is relevant for a new urban development paradigm because it integrates as many aspects of the food system as possible into a local production and consumption cycle. Commercially, this is beneficial since there are few intermediates. In terms of freshness, taste and nutrition, food goes directly to consumers and restaurant customers. From Your Own City is looking to deploy its professional food production chain to less connected urban locations throughout the Netherlands, creating local food hubs in various cities.

....

www.uitjeeigenstad.nl

Varkenshuis (The Pig House)
Tilburg city centre, Rotterdam city centre, and the small village of Annerveenschekanaal, the Netherlands

....

Starting date
2012 - 2013

Status
In progress

....

....

The Pig House is both a pigsty and a house in which to gather, eat, drink and talk. A Pig House is built by a local community with local materials, with the initial concept coming from an idea by Elles Kiers and Sjef Muijman. Every community builds its own unique Pig House, with local materials in the local style. The Pig House has room for two pigs that are fed on leftovers from the local community. When ready, the pigs will be butchered and eaten by the locals who took care of them.

The pig is traditionally the 'savings bank' of the family. In times of abundance (harvest time) the pig shared the leftovers and kitchen waste of its caretakers. In times of scarcity (winter time) the butchered pig provided food. The number of pigs that were kept depended on the food available for them, with food surplus in times of plenty being transformed into pork to be eaten in times of scarcity. The system worked well, and the Pig House aims to rebalance these needs and yields.

The Pig House reintroduces both the age-old tradition of keeping pigs and the sharing of responsibility with neighbours for animals that are the community's joint future nourishment. This requires the community to work together for mutual benefit.

The experience of taking care of the pigs will be captured in words and images, and shared with the public on specially created plates. In this way, the project is both a performance and a practical investigation.

Zuidpark Urban Farming Rooftop
Amsterdam, the Netherlands

. . . .

Starting date
June 2012

Status
In progress

. . . .

. . . .

Zuidpark Urban Farming Rooftop sits on the roof of a modernist office building that has recently been renovated to offer flexible, mobile working facilities. The rooftop has several functions: it serves as the office park, where people can meet, walk, and eat lunch. It is also a cultivation space where 70 different fruits, vegetables and herbs are grown. The food is harvested by cooks who prepare food at one of the building's lunch corners, and also by office workers wanting to take fresh produce home for dinner.

Zuidpark shows that urban farming is as much about adding amenity, as well as social and economic value, to an office building as it is about cultivation. A non-traditional office environment has been created, not only because the building fosters sustainable entrepreneurship and provides flexible workspace, but also because it incorporates the rooftop farm into its operational concept, providing welcome additional space in an increasingly dense urban environment. Even smart working practices thrive on face-to-face contact, and the rooftop farm functions as an attractive meeting place for employees from the various companies renting office space in the building.

. . . .

www.zuidpark.nl

The Selection in Numbers

The projects showcased in our collection represent but a few of the pioneering developments being taken forward today, many by grass roots groups operating, at least initially, without formal public or private funding. Many are concerned simply with raising awareness, while others directly impact on community life, education, economic viability and access to healthy food. While we did not specifically search for the latest or most media-friendly schemes, all demonstrate the growing trend for engagement with food-related urban initiatives and all except one were founded in or after 2007.

Ideally, food-related projects have multiple beneficial effects on urban life: a desirable output rooted in the key permaculture concept of 'stacking', or obtaining multiple yields from any single element in a system. By design, most project initiators understand the exponential effect of combining urban activities, organisations, people, infrastructure and funding streams. For example, 22 out of the 34 projects featured benefit urban infrastructure in terms of creating or improving food growing sites or transport systems. Almost as many are exemplary in an environmental sense, practicing closed-cycle production and consumption loops, efficient water and energy management, and effective soil remediation. Health and livability benefits are key outputs in 20 projects; education and awareness-raising in 15. The social and economic significance of food projects is a focus for 14 projects, demonstrating how food-related initiatives create jobs, empower the less well-off, strengthen communities and contribute to economic viability.

The scope of this collection of projects gives an accurate impression of the many ways in which urban food initiatives can be not only ends in themselves, but also means for creating a better urban world. Our aim is simply to inspire: to show citizens, practitioners, designers, activists, artists and policymakers the incredible potential of food as a tool for enhancing our social, economic and physical urban environments.

URBAN IMPACT OF THE PROJECTS

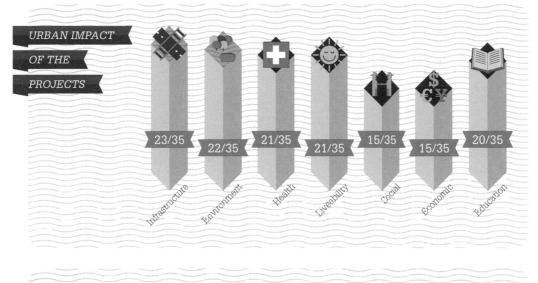

Infrastructure	Environment	Health	Liveability	Social	Economic	Education
23/35	22/35	21/35	21/35	15/35	15/35	20/35

URBAN LOCATION

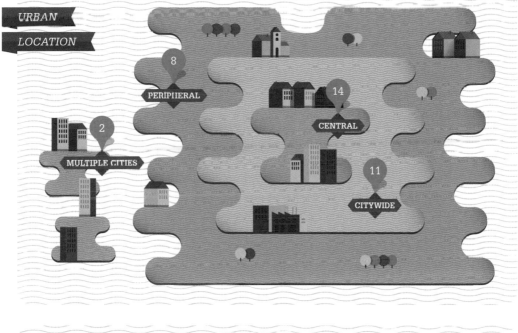

- 8 PERIPHERAL
- 2 MULTIPLE CITIES
- 14 CENTRAL
- 11 CITYWIDE

STARTING DATE

1982	2007	2007	2009	2010	2011	2012	2013
1	1	2	4	4	7	15	1

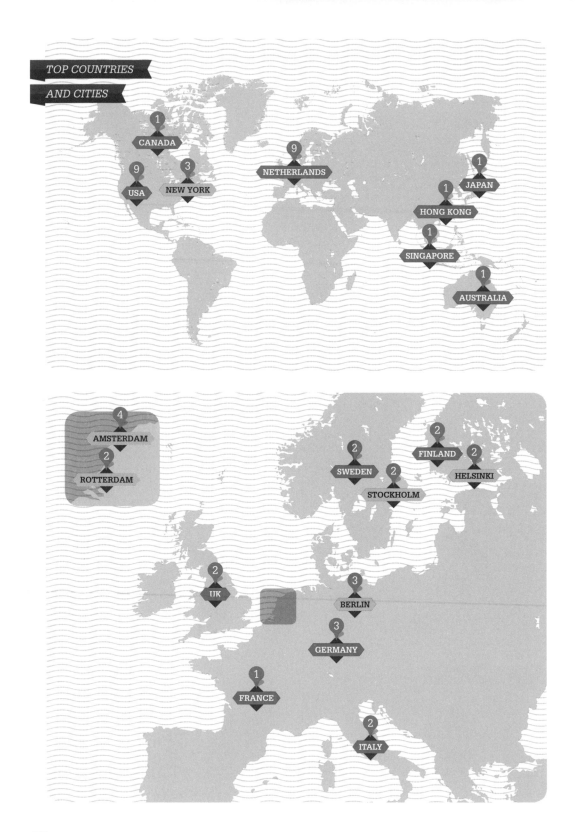

TOP COUNTRIES
AND CITIES

CANADA 1

USA 9

NEW YORK 3

NETHERLANDS 9

JAPAN 1

HONG KONG 1

SINGAPORE 1

AUSTRALIA 1

AMSTERDAM 4

ROTTERDAM 2

SWEDEN 2

STOCKHOLM 2

FINLAND 2

HELSINKI 2

UK 2

BERLIN 3

GERMANY 3

FRANCE 1

ITALY 2

Epilogue

Food as a Tool – an Epilogue

As suggested in the introduction to this book, the thoughts and experience within represent an exploration of current realities in the area of local food practice. Thanks to contributions from a forward-thinking and pioneering team of international experts, we have created a book that elevates urban agriculture from a collection of food production experiences into an organised process that localises the complete food cycle.

Just as the food cycle brings together people, practice and skills to create true urban innovation, with these concluding remarks we go beyond collated knowledge and define a new paradigm: food as a tool for urban development. We will re-visit and re-use the notion of *field* as a means to understand urban communities under conditions of rapid social and political change, and analyse the impact of such social flux on urban life. We will re-define local food movements, initiatives, institutions and networks in terms of *local food fields*, and introduce suggestions about how local food fields can be used to (re)plan the built environment, (re)connect the divided city and boost offline sociality.

The Concept of Field in Urban Development

We aim to reframe the food movement. In order to do that, we must understand the socio-economic circumstances and patterns characterising food-related practice in the 21st century, along with the theoretical underpinnings of the new framework we aim to introduce. The concept of 'field' was originally used in the 1950s by cultural anthropologists to characterise periods of rapid social transition, with new affiliations being continually made and remade around emerging occupational and recreational practices. More recently, the field concept has been effectively used by Allen Scott and other urban researchers when analysing the rise of creative industries at the beginning of the 2000s. The concept of 'creative field' followed; a tool to analyse the wave of innovative creative and cultural industries that emerged to employ generations of well-educated and artistic professionals across the de-industrialised cities of the global north. As the new millennium took shape, it became clear to policymakers that the products and services delivered by these new industries were imbued with social and economic 'added value'. Cultural and creative activities were suddenly taken more seriously in terms of economic development and their ability to embed local identity. Simultaneously, the growth and professionalization of these industries took place on a massive scale.

Many urban explorers had noted the unexplored potential of these undefined and loosely connected activities as urban economic drivers. The transformation of such local creative enterprise into an identifiable economic powerhouse known as 'the creative industries' formed the core of a new discourse in urban development. Cities eager to stimulate and regenerate under-performing neighbourhoods began creating favourable conditions to attract creative businesses. This process illustrates that all kinds of loosely connected activities – in this case those linked by a creative focus – have spatial, economic

and social articulations which can be framed by the notion
of *field*.

....

Defining the Local Food Field

During its three-year journey, the Farming the City project's
involvement with local food systems led to a focus on food-
related entrepreneurship, its connection to urban demand,
its spatial articulation and its social interdependence. As our
approach to food-related activities became more comprehensive
we realised that, then as now, informal local food systems are
not well organised. While the traditional global food supply
chain fills our supermarkets daily with alarming efficiency
(urban planners need to accept their share of responsibility for
creating 'food deserts' due to infrastructure planning practices
that have not moved on from destructive modernist thinking[1]),
the supply of local products is frequently inefficient, fragmented
and, in many cases, actually adds to urban congestion. Many
local food processing and packaging systems are 'one-offs' that
cannot be replicated to deliver economies of scale. Local food
systems are in a stage of initial disorder, but food as an issue
reaches deep into so many areas of public life – health,
economy, environment, politics, the social and cultural spheres
– that a wide range of professionals are now working to
determine possible trajectories for future development.

The projects featured in the book demonstrate the magnificent
variety of innovative ideas flourishing across what we allow
ourselves to define as the *food field*. As urban researchers, we
are primed to seek similarities, differences and patterns. It
seems obvious that there is a degree of similarity between the
articulation (spatial, social and economic) of today's emerging
food field and the creative field of the early 2000s. These include
recognition of the potential of underused urban spaces, the
engagement of local communities and the positive impact

of food-related activities on community cohesion and communication.

The food field is helping to fill urban voids, both physical and social ones. This process is directly comparable to the way creativity played out its role in urban development; re-vitalising underused spaces in ways that would have been problematic for more traditional industries. The food field is also adjusting the shape and form of agricultural activities – which over the past century have become bloated and disconnected from the local context – to a more human scale.

Another similarity is the emergence of urban networks and communities. In many Western cities, the creative 'scene' has claimed a key share of the urban economy. It has developed its own economic structures (supply chains), networks and communities of practice (communities with shared values, narratives and language). The same process is now happening with the food field: driven by the reality of providing for growing demand. The creative industries provided services and products with a relatively high 'sign value' (its value within a system of objects, for example, one handbag may have no additional functional benefits over another, but may signify commonly understood higher 'prestige') compared to its functional value (what things actually do). Therefore, the level of economic activity derived from ideas and products with high symbolic and aesthetic values (those from graphic design, advertising and fashion design), has risen dramatically in many cities.

The food field is currently experiencing such a trend. Since healthy, 'fair' and locally sourced food has become symbolically important to a growing group of (urban) consumers, there is an expanding market for urban food projects. This creates an opportunity for the food field to make up a larger share of the urban economy.

Cluster Benefits for the Local Food Field

In the first decade of the 21st century, following a growing awareness of the economic potential inherent in the creative industries, 'boosting' or fostering culture and creativity became a key urban growth strategy for many Western cities. Numerous policymakers, social researchers and geographers proclaimed the increasing importance of creativity, culture and knowledge as the driving forces of urban economies and city regeneration across the global north. Public policy, funds and support were redirected towards anything that could be construed as cultural or creative (the European capitals of culture, for example, or English music as an urban catalyst in Liverpool, Manchester, Berlin and Amsterdam, where subsidised work and living space was given to artists in specific neighbourhoods. In seeking a development path for the urban food field, the analysis of this process becomes extremely interesting from two perspectives. One, a focus on how creative industries have (been) physically grouped together in order to encourage and stimulate collaboration, cross-fertilisation and inter-disciplinary working. Two, a keen interest in critically understanding the impact of this process, and whether the food field can follow a similar trajectory.

Many urban policies have focused on grouping together industries with similar areas of interest, thereby creating urban *clusters*, often known as 'districts' or 'quarters' (fashion, design, art, culture, music … you name it). The concepts of *field* and *cluster* are inspirational. They enable consideration of how to 'order' the emerging chaotic existence of local food innovation in our cities. In reference to clustering theory, it is possible to foresee that a functioning *food field* will rely on local products and small-scale, fine-grained industries. It will be organised around local funding streams and will rely on the local community for all aspects of production, including packaging and transportation, as well as for consumption.

Food clustering can aggregate, both vertically and horizontally, several small-scale local food industries (production, transport, processing, packaging and waste/recycling). Educational and research institutions will grow to foster and support this aggregation. Eventually, because an important by-product of spatial proximity is high symbolic value and a coherent identity, this clustering will become a catalyst of urban development, investments, eco-tourism and environmental awareness.

In analysing this process it is apparent that, at the beginning of the 2000s, many young people were employed by the emergent creative industries. While this can be seen as having a positive effect on the local economy, it is also true that such prospects are effectively available to only a specific social grouping (typically well-educated and affluent cultural professionals, or those involved with the arts). This results in a societal dichotomy which tends to exclude the less well-educated or less well-skilled workforce. Although this excluded workforce is sometimes employed by emerging support services (laundry, service, cleaning), such jobs are dependent on the success of the industries that spawn them. This dichotomy has visible spatial effects: it becomes clear that using creativity as a 'magic solution' for urban development can lead to spatial segregation whereby specific groups are increasingly excluded from the dominant urban planning discourse. Typically, those displaced are less affluent and more vulnerable; frequently welfare-dependent, chronically under-employed and thus severely disadvantaged by their inability to integrate into the new social order.

Such social segregation creates divided cities. With culture and creativity acting as the currency of urban makeover, only certain groups are invited to participate in the new economy. In many cases, the creative field did not take into account the need to accommodate the complete social spectrum.[2] The food field, however, *can* and *will* be different. Food, by nature, is a basic need that all human beings share and a currency that all have access to. Food can become a vital connection that transcends cultural, economic and social boundaries.

In essence, this means using food as a tool. It means going beyond the basic idea of harnessing local food production to feed our cities. Contemporary cities are nodes in a network of relationships. Global interconnectivity has made it possible for many cities to flourish, but has also disconnected them from local food systems.[3] We believe that this process is too embedded on a global scale to unpick. What we need to focus on and pay attention to now is local context and local challenges.

Surely, the smaller the challenge, the easier it is to overcome? Yet what is more problematic, both intellectually and practically, is using food as a means to create opportunities for all. By approaching food as a *process* instead of a product, we can frame it as a tool to support distinctive local traits (economic strengths, networks, communities, natural resources). According to social and economic geographers, regional economies benefit from the clustering of small-scale activities. Clustering can be especially successful when it is rooted in local economic, cultural, and institutional assets. A successful cluster cannot be easily created out of nothing, but rather must support, foster and connect existing local traits and qualities.[4]

Such thinking can be readily applied to the local food field, especially when connecting it to the large quantities of food produced at the fringes of most cities in the global north. Food activities and networks are present in every city. Moreover, by approaching civil society as a means of employment[5], it is possible to rethink neighbourhoods and districts as production, processing and recycling machines. In this scenario, skilled and unskilled professionals work together in a collaborative system to meet the needs and aspirations of the local community, to use and re-use resources and to innovate, experiment and observe.

This is particularly relevant because such activity can help to fill the political and practical voids created by governments that have, over past decades, increasingly retreated from civil society. As the dismantling of the welfare state in many countries continues, embedding societal demands within local economies could well be part of a new civil solution.[6]

....

Recommendations and Proposals

In this book, we have positioned our ideas and our practice in an emerging theoretical framework. Still, it remains necessary to define some clear directives about *how* to use food as a tool for urban development. The book has been divided into three sections, each of which tackles a particular issue. The first section explores ways in which policy makers and urban designers can work together in order to re-think urban food, energy and waste cycles, urban infrastructure and urban flows. The key notion is the disconnect in today's municipal structures: the (partial) localisation of food cycles is a multidisciplinary process that requires a political and societal shift. Transforming urban green into edible green, advocating an inclusive food policy and supporting the development of food-related infrastructures (in buildings and outside them, together with sustainable, water-based or electric transport to connect with regional producers) are some examples of the changes that a well-considered food policy could initiate.

The second section of the book addresses the relationship between an emerging economic system and the social topography of western cities. Economic models are shifting towards diversified systems with the potential to support new business cases. These models will foster local entrepreneurship and act as enablers for low-income communities in terms of production and consumption cycles.

The third section of the book addresses people. Citizens, artists and social workers are exploring different ways to facilitate and enable community cohesion and resilience across our divided cities. There is clearly a great need for initiatives that can create the conditions needed to encourage urban communities to communicate, collaborate and connect; to inspire each other and work together for common goals.

The final section of the book brings together ideas, innovation, concepts, theories and stories. It celebrates the many and varied ways in which food-related activity is already improving cities across the world. The projects showcased here represent only a glimpse of what the near future may have in store for us, but are nonetheless an inspiring collection that will alert aspiring food activists, entrepreneurs, policymakers and designers as to what is already possible.

Taken together, the concepts that we have explored create a framework that outlines how food can be used as a tool for urban development.

_Re-planning the built environment: in order to create a more localised and sustainable food system, we should take a good look at what is already available and build on that, making every possible use of existing assets. Under-used urban areas and buildings, existing facades and roof terraces have all been hailed as future food production zones in many books and publications. However, we go further, insisting on appropriate contextualisation. Western cities typically consist of either compact or sprawling agglomerations within a 'green belt' of agricultural/productive lands. Farmers in many Western countries are subsidised by state funds because of increasing imbalance and massive global competition across agricultural markets.

Surely there is a better way? The developing evidence base suggests that it is far more productive to create sustainable infrastructure and enable traditional food producers to re-connect with local markets. Each city can have its local food supply chain. The challenge is to embed sustainability and resilience into the operational framework, helping local farmers to re-think their business models and logistics and adapt to a new, less globally dependent order. Transport, packaging and processing systems can all be localised.

_Bridging the gaps between urban citizens: food is a connector, and the implementation of innovative ways to produce, transport and package local food can create employment and foster cohesion. When re-using abandoned industrial sites, or redeveloping the waterfront, consider the development of food infrastructure that can provide opportunities for local communities.

_Increase offline cohesion: the act of growing food in the urban environment should not be seen only as an emergent economic paradigm. Local food production is, without doubt, one of the most powerful forces for re-establishing community; of encouraging people to look outside their houses and away from their screens. There are countless examples of the positive effects of food cultivation on physical and psychological health. Many educational and social programmes have already been implemented; it is a no-brainer to stress the incredible potential of local food systems to help humanise, connect and socialise our urban populations.

Conclusion

Much has been written about food systems, how they impact on living environments and how we should try to improve them. As we suggested in the introduction to this book, local food systems are being re-invented across the global north. Traditional food supply processes have become disconnected from cities during the past two centuries. The inexorable process of change, supposedly representing advancement, modernisation and progress, can be viewed in a different light when considering its many negative impacts on urban development, health, nutrition and well-being.

The key question is: how can innovative food initiatives contribute to the re-interpretation and reshaping of urban dynamics in a physical, economic, social, and technological sense? By exploring the wider theoretical concept of economic clustering, food-related businesses, local economies, communities and small-scale farmers can be re-positioned into the local food field. Within a cooperative framework, a process of vertical integration (where production, transport, processing, packaging and waste are part of the same virtuous circle) could inform resilient (post-deindustrialisation, post-creative, post-crisis) urban strategies to pave the way to carbon light living.

New research would no doubt further our understanding of the concept of the food field. However, this book does not propose an on-going academic process. Academic knowledge has been effectively used to frame and understand emerging food practices, but the immediate need at this stage is for *practice*. We need more citizens' initiatives, more experiments, more mistakes, more failures and more successes. We hope that this book will inspire urban communities to rise to the challenge of transition. Living well in urban communities is an incredibly complex undertaking, and we need to aim for more flexible, adaptable and resilient ways of fulfilling our many needs.

References

··········

**Feeding the City: the Challenge
of Urban Food Planning**
Kevin Morgan

1   American Planning Association (2007) *Policy Guide on
    Community and Regional Food Planning,* APA

2   Viljoen, A (ed.) (2005) *Continuous Productive Urban
    Landscapes: Designing Urban Agriculture for Sustainable
    Cities,* Architectural Press, London

3   Lang, T, Barling, D and Caraher, M (2009) *Food Policy:
    Integrating Health, Environment and Society,* Oxford
    University Press, Oxford

4   Morgan, K and Sonnino, R (2010) The Urban Foodscape:
    World Cities and the New Food Equation, *Cambridge
    Journal of Regions, Economy and Society,* 3(2), pp. 209-224

5   FAO (2000) *Food for the Cities: A Briefing Guide for Mayors,
    City Executives and Urban Planners in Developing
    Countries and Countries in Transition,* FAO, Rome

6   IFPRI (2009) *2009 Global Hunger Index,* IFPRI,
    Washington DC

7   Morgan, K, Marsden, T and Murdoch, J (2006) *Worlds
    of Food: Place, Power and Provenance in the Food Chain,*
    Oxford University Press, Oxford

8   Born, B and Purcell, (2006) Avoiding the Local Trap:
    Scale and Food Systems in Planning Research, *Journal
    of Planning Education and Research,* Volume 26 (2),
    pp. 195-207

9   Morgan, K (2010) Local and Green, Global and Fair: The
    Ethical Foodscape and the Politics of Care, *Environment
    and Planning A,* 42(8), pp. 1852-1867

··········

Urban Agriculture: Designing the Productive City
Katrin Bohn/Andre Viljoen

1   Bohn, K. and Viljoen, A. (2010) *Continuous Productive Urban
    Landscape (CPUL): Designing essential infrastructure,*
    Beijing: Landscape Architecture China, pp. 24-30

2   Viljoen, A., Bohn. K. and Pena Diaz, J. (2004) *London
    Thames Gateway: Proposals for implementing CPULs
    in London Riverside and the Lower Lea Valley,* Brighton:
    University of Brighton publication

3   Jansma, J. E. and Visser, A.J. (2011) *Agromere: Integrating
    urban agriculture in the development of the city of Almere,*
    Leusden: Urban Agriculture Magazine, no. 25, pp. 28-31

4   Wageningen UR (2011) *Agromere.* Available at:
    http://www.agromere.wur.nl/UK (accessed 14 July 2012)

5   Jansma, J. E. and Visser, A.J. (2011) *Agromere: Integrating
    urban agriculture in the development of the city of Almere,*
    Leusden: Urban Agriculture Magazine, no. 25, pp. 28-31

6   Growing Power, Inc. (2010) *Growing Power,* Available at:
    http://www.growingpower.org (accessed 14 July 2012)

7   Eastern Market Corporation (2007) *Detroit Eastern Market,*
    Available at: http://www.detroiteasternmarket.com
    (accessed 14 July 2012)

8   Spiel/Feld Marzahn (2011) *Spiel/Feld Marzahn,* Available
    at: http://www.spielfeldmarzahn.de (accessed 14 july 2012)

9   Bohn, K., Ritzmann, K. and Awan, N. (2012) *Spiel/Feld
    Urbane Landwirtschaft: Praxisorientiertes Entwerfen und
    Oekologische Bildung,* Berlin: self-published for the local
    government of Berlin – Marzahn-Hellersdorf

10 The London Assembly (2010) *Cultivating the Capital:
    Food growing and the planning system in London,* London:
    The London Assembly

11 Nomadisch Grün gGmbH (2009) *Prinzessinnengärten,*
    Available at: http://prinzessinnengarten.net (accessed 2012)

12 Gallagher, J. (2010) *Reimagining Detroit: Opportunities for
    Redefining an American City,* Painted Turtle Book, Detroit

··········

Future Foodscapes
Jan-Willem van der Schans

1   Steel, C. (2009) *Hungry City: How Food Shapes Our Lives.*
    Random House, London

2   Wiskerke, J.S.C. (2009) On places lost and places regained:
    reflections on the alternative food geography and
    sustainable regional development, *International Planning
    Studies,* 14 (4), pp. 369-387

3   Cronon, W. (1992) *Nature's Metropolis: Chicago and the
    Great West.* WW. Norton & Company, New York

4   Thünen, J. von (1826) *Der Isolierte Staat in Beziehung auf
    landwirtschaft und Nationalekonomie.* Fischer, Jena.

5   Sinclair, J. (1966) Beginning the Study of Lexis, in C. E.
    Bazell, J. C. Catford, M. A. K. Halliday, and R. H. Robins
    (eds.): *In Memory of J. R. Firth.* Longman

··········

Local Food, Fresh and Fair
Oran B Hesterman

1   http://www.fns.usda.gov/pd/29snapcurrpp.htm, http://
    farmersmarketcoalition.org/snap-redemptions-at-farmers-
    markets-exceed-11m-in-2011

2   http://www.bcise.com/Guides/Sept-2010/55-Sustainable3.
    pdf; http://www.ams.usda.gov/AMSv1.0/ams.
    fetchTemplateData.do?template=TemplateS&leftNav=
    WholesaleandFarmersMarkets&page=WFMFarmersMarket
    Growth&description=Farmers%20Market%20
    Growth&acct=frmrdirmkt

....

3 'Food, Conservation, and Energy Act of 2008,' 110th Cong., 2nd sess., http://www.govtrack.us/congress/bill.xpd?bill-h110-6124

4 Mari Gallagher Research & Consulting Group, 'Examining the Impact of Food Deserts in Chicago' (2006), p. 30, Chicago

5 You can see their interaction on Fair Food Network's Youtube channel: http://www.youtube.com/watch?v=aoHM11PGPKg&feature=plcp

6 Michigan Department of Community Health, Michigan Behavioral Risk Factor Survey

7 Centers for Disease Control and Prevention, High School Youth Risk Behavior Survey

8 Michigan Department of Community Health, Michigan Behavioral Risk Factor Survey

9 Michael Shuman, 'Economic Impact of Localizing Detroit's Food System,' www.fairfoodnetwork.org/resources/economic-impact-localizing-detroits-food-system

10 Double Up Food Bucks 2011 Evaluation Report. http://www.fairfoodnetwork.org/resources/double-food-bucks-2011-evaluation-report

11 http://www.wkkf.org/news/Articles/2012/05/Americans-overwhelmingly-support-doubling-food-stamp-value-at-farmers-markets.aspx

12 For more information, visit http://www.doubleupfoodbucks.org

....

Possibilities and Pitfalls: Urban Food Security
Jennifer Sumner, JJ McMurtry and Michael Classens

1 Classens, Michael, McMurtry JJ and Sumner, Jennifer. 2013 (forthcoming). "Doing Markets Differently: The Case of FoodShare Toronto's Good Food Markets." In Jack Quarter and Sherida Ryan (eds.). *Social Purpose Enterprises: Case Studies in Doing Business Differently.* University of Toronto Press, Toronto

....

Tokyo, a Fruitful City
Chris Berthelsen/Jared Braiterman/Jess Mantell

1 Jinnai, H. (1995). Tokyo; A Spatial Anthropology. trans. Kimiko Nishimura. University of California Press, Berkeley and Los Angeles, California. (pp. 134-135)

2 Dense Edo – 688 people per hectare compared with 250 in 1994. In the Nagaya of Edo class structures (external, economic, intellectual, artistic) overlapped, resulting in a vital mix of ages, classes, and professions. See Chapter 4 of Kurokawa, K. (1994). Philosophy of Symbiosis. John Wiley & Sons

3 Adjusted quote from Kurokawa (1994: Chapter 4)

4 DeRoo, R.J. (2006). Extracts from 'Annette Messager's Images of the Everyday: The Feminist Recasting of '68', in The Museum Establishment and Contemporary Art: The Politics of Artistic Display in France after 1968. Cambridge, England, Cambridge University Press

5 Hat tip to Ivan Illich

6 Which is not surprising given that Japan is neck-and-neck with Korea for the title of world's second largest persimmon producer

7 Tsukamoto Yoshiharu, quoted in Kitayama, K. 2010c. An interview with Yoshiharu Tsukamoto. In Tokyo Metabolizing. TOTO Publishing, Tokyo, pp. 67-73

8 See Carson, K.A. (2009). The Homebrew Industrial Revolution. Center for a Stateless Society Paper No. 5 (September 2009). Available from http://c4ss.org/wp-content/uploads/2009/09/C4SS-Desktop-Manufacturing.pdf, especially page 6

9 Links to examples that are drawn from our survey of blogs and online forums can be found at http://a-small-lab.com/farming-the-city-links.html

10 See Masao (2004) Delivering the Goods. entrepreneurship and innovation in a Japanese corporation (LTCB International Library Trust, Kokusai Bunka Kaikan) for an in-depth look at how Japan's pioneer courier service Yamato Takkyubin impacted lives, lifestyles and business in Japan

....

Food as a Tool – an Epilogue

1 Morgan, M. and R. Sonnino (2010) The Urban Foodscape: World Cities and the New Food Equation, *Cambridge Journal of Regions, Economy and Society,* 3, pp. 209-224

2 Krätke, S. (2012) 'Creative cities' and the rise of the dealer class, in: Brenner, N., P. Marcuse and M. Mayer (eds.) *Cities for People, Not for Profit.* Routledge, London

3 Wiskerke, J.S.C. (2009) On Places Lost and Places Regained: Reflections on the Alternative Food Geography and Sustainable Regional Development, *International Planning Studies,* (14) 4, pp. 369-387

4 Turok, I (2009) The Distinctive City: Pitfalls in the Pursuit of Differential Advantage, Environment and Planning A 41(1), pp. 13-30

5 Rifkin (2011) *The Third Industrial Revolution: How Lateral Power is Transforming Energy, the Economy, and the World.* Palgrave MacMillan, London

6 00:/ (2012) *Compendium for the Civic Economy.* trancityxvaliz, Haarlem

Credits of the images